D0809270

A G.I.'s Vietnam Diary

A G.I.'s Vietnam Diary

✦

A JOURNEY THROUGH MYSELF

Dominick Yezzo

Edited By:
Ellen M Cooney

iUniverse, Inc.
New York Lincoln Shanghai

A G.I.'s Vietnam Diary
A JOURNEY THROUGH MYSELF

Copyright © 1974, 2006 by Dominick Yezzo

All rights reserved. No part of this book may be used or reproduced by any means, graphic, electronic, or mechanical, including photocopying, recording, taping or by any information storage retrieval system without the written permission of the publisher except in the case of brief quotations embodied in critical articles and reviews.

iUniverse books may be ordered through booksellers or by contacting:

iUniverse
2021 Pine Lake Road, Suite 100
Lincoln, NE 68512
www.iuniverse.com
1-800-Authors (1-800-288-4677)

ISBN 0-531-02684-1
ORIGINALLY PUBLISHED BY FRANKLIN WATTS, INC NEW YORK 1974
COPYRIGHT 1974 BY DOMINICK YEZZO

ISBN-13: 978-0-595-39250-6 (pbk)
ISBN-13: 978-0-595-83644-4 (ebk)
ISBN-10: 0-595-39250-4 (pbk)
ISBN-10: 0-595-83644-5 (ebk)

Printed in the United States of America

This book is

Affectionately dedicated to

My late mother and father

And the rest of the world

In hope of love, reason, and understanding...

"We shall laugh again,
but we shall never be young again."

—Dominick Yezzo

"Death in war is the same now as it always has been."

—Dominick Yezzo

"Lord, make me an instrument of your peace.
Where there is hatred, let me sow love.
Where there is injury; pardon.
Where there is doubt; faith.
Where there is despair, hope.
When there is darkness; light.
Where there is sadness; joy."

—Francis of Assisi

AUTHOR'S NOTE

In 1968, I embarked upon a long journey…a journey through myself. I learned that it is each man's war as he sees it through his own eyes and as he thinks it to be through his own mind.

I was very young when I went to war. I had not yet been able to form convictions about anything. I had nothing but an innate responsibility to those I came in contact with.

I went away to Vietnam sad but I had faith because my parents and teachers taught me that America was as solid as a rock. I was also taught to believe in America and its policies. I am sorry to report that sometimes I can no longer feel that.

I see myself in this account as an ordinary boy from the United States of America who was thrust into a violent and senseless situation caused by his government. As a soldier called upon to serve that government, I was soon forced to know my own capabilities and limitations. In so doing, I began to question myself and my country. In the end, I was left with a feeling of horror and confusion. I have since tried to mold these feelings into a firm stand against the ills and injustices in American society.

I love America, as I am certain most Americans do in their own hearts. The progress and technology that has taken place in this action in the last two hundred years is almost incredible. The United States of America is indeed a science fiction land come true. We have taken concrete, metals, glass and other materials from the earth and transformed them into buildings, airplanes, automobiles, and other products of peace. But we have also taken those same materials and manufactured them into the tools of war.

Unfortunately, there are definite elements of selfishness, greed, and corruption inherent in America. These maim and confuse our society, cause resentment and suspicion, and are ultimately responsible for marching men off to war. All too often it is those in power who are impelled by these elements. It is my belief that they have no right to spend lives for economic development and monetary gain. I urge those in power to correct these evils. For is it not up to each and every living person to conduct his life in a manner befitting every other living person? Are we not all tiny specks of life contributing to the vast whole of nature?

In this spirit, I give this journal to you as a true account of my experience. It is a very personal account—a gut reaction to the Vietnamese war as I saw it. To those who read it, I hope I can stir in them an honest quest for all things good.

God bless you.

Dominick Yezzo

I would like to thank the many people who have—over the years—encouraged me to put this book back in print.

Many thanks to Patricia Cooney for proof reading.

Information for historical references was researched from Wikipedia.com, The New York Times archives, and The BBC archives

Aug 14, 1968

I left home this morning and have begun my long and unyielding military trip to Vietnam. Where the war is.

Last night, I was out with Jennifer, my girl friend. I thought I wanted to be with her on that final evening at home. Now I don't know. Dad didn't wait up for me, so I didn't get a chance to see him before my departure. He left a note, though. Maybe I shouldn't have gone out.

My brothers, Jimmy, Frank, and Wayne, took me to the airport and saw me off. It was raining out at Kennedy and I felt horrible leaving them.

After the plane took off, I felt the cold reality of what was happening to me. I was leaving New York, my home in the United States. I was being transported to Vietnam as a soldier.

As the plane flew westward I was thinking: I don't feel ready for this. I don't understand it. Is the short basic training I've been through at Fort Jackson, South Carolina enough? Will I be expected to shoot at people? Will I be able to maintain myself?

Maybe I've been a fool. A few months before, I was offered a chance at Officers' Candidate School. I refused because it would have meant signing up for an additional year to receive more training. Later, I was offered a chance to become a helicopter pilot. But I didn't pass the medical exam for pilots' school because I don't have perfect vision and must wear glasses.

So I wound up at Fort Jackson taking standard Army basic training. When it was over, they lined us up and called a lot of guys out of formation. All of them called were given orders to proceed to Vietnam. I wasn't one of them. A friend and I were given orders to report to Fort Detrick, Maryland, an Army Chemical and Biological Warfare Research Center.

I was told that procedures for a secret clearance were underway for me.

At Fort Detrick, I was a driver for doctors and scientists, generals and colonels who were involved in the study of germ warfare and defoliation processes. I drove them to and from the Pentagon and National, Friendship, and Dulles Airports.

But it didn't last at Detrick. With the intensive buildup of military forces in Vietnam, the Army rummaged through their files and cleaned out all personnel who hadn't served a tour of duty in Southeast Asia. I received orders to report to Fort Lewis, Washington, for my transferal to Vietnam, and was given a two-week leave. And now, here I am on this airplane headed to the war.

Later, same day

I arrived at Seattle and took a room at the Olympia Hotel. I had a drink and walked down and took my first look at the Pacific Ocean. Then I visited the remains of the past World's Fair that had been held here.

The khaki uniform Mom pressed for me wasn't as fresh looking as it was this morning, but I didn't care. Tonight I had a good time in Seattle by myself.

AUG
15

I took a Greyhound bus to Fort Lewis, one of the processing centers for Vietnam-bound G.I.s. Have been issued jungle gear and all of the Army necessities except a rifle. Been pulling so many details, K.P., cleanup, etc.

AUG
17

My group left today via DC-8 commercial jet. We stopped in Hawaii, then made a non-scheduled stop at Wake Island because some tall, thin kid was so nervous he got sick and passed out. They said he even stopped breathing. He was a brand new bridegroom, had been married only a week.

Next stop was at the Philippines.

I began to get tense when we boarded the plane this time. Next stop-the war.

AUG
18

Have arrived at Cam Ranh Bay, South Vietnam. The heat hit me hard in the face.

I anticipated seeing war, whatever it is, as soon as I got off the plane, but it wasn't like that. I saw some fighter jets take off and then we were put on buses and taken to another processing center. Cam Ranh Bay is a sandy peninsula and harbor. U.S. government supply lines keep it heavy with traffic, both air and sea. Because it is surrounded by water on three sides, it is one of the most secure places in Vietnam.

I'm not afraid. I realize that I'm not an infantry soldier. I saw some Vietnamese women washing G.I. clothing. I stood and stared at them for a while and they giggled.

I have been assigned to the 1st Air Cavalry Division. I'm told it's a tough crack unit, with the most helicopter support. I saw a few "choppers" buzzing around today; quite a machine.

NEWS FROM THE U.S....

Upheaval at Democratic Convention in Chicago:

The assassination of popular candidate Robert F. Kennedy looms. Democrats are split over the Vietnam War. Eugene McCarthy's campaign is anti-war, calling for immediate withdrawal. Hubert H. Humphrey, in line with President Lyndon Johnson's policy, focused on making any reduction of force contingent on concessions of the Paris Peace Talks.

Anti-war demonstrators protested. Scenes of police beating up peaceful protestors and reporters received widespread coverage on television. Mayor Richard J. Daley took a hard line against the protesters, refusing permits for rallies and marches, and calling for whatever use of force necessary to subdue the crowds. U.S. Sen. Ribicoff (D-Conn.) infuriated Daley by saying, "with George McGovern as President of the United States, we wouldn't have Gestapo tactics in the streets of Chicago." Lipreaders and eyewitnesses contended that Daley responded by saying "Get off the stage you fucking kike!" Daley claimed he was yelling "You faker!"

Protesters, including Abbie Hoffman, Tom Hayden, and Dave Dellinger, known as the "Chicago Eight", were, on February 18, 1970, found guilty of conspiring to incite riots, but charges were eventually dismissed on appeal.

A federal commission (The Walker Report to the National Commission on the Causes and Prevention of Violence) later described the incident as a "police riot," implicitly blaming Daley for inciting the police to commit violence.

AUG
23

Left Cam Ranh Bay with the other G.I.s assigned to the 1st Air Cavalry. We flew via C-123 Military Airlift Command to a place called An Khe in the Central Highlands. An Khe is the rear element base camp of my unit.

This heat is knocking me out. The food is hardly fit to eat. More processing and more details.

This base camp is huge. There are many hutches (small temporary buildings made of wire screen), lots of trucks and jeeps running around, an airstrip-and a P.X., much to my surprise. Barbed wire and concertina wire form a perimeter, and there are bunkers about every twenty yards. The bunkers are guard posts with M-60 machine guns, grenade launchers, Claymore mines, etc. G.I.s are on constant watch in the bunkers.

Inside the barbed wire is American; outside is "Charlie."[1]

AUG
24

I've been assigned to the Civil Affairs and Psychological Operations Branch (G-5) of the 1st Air Cavalry. I'm going to Camp Evans, a base camp north of the city of Hue, close to the D.M.Z. (Demilitarized Zone).

The mission of this section is finding out enemy positions and dropping propaganda leaflets over them. Broadcasting to the enemy from choppers is also one of our unit's primary functions. I miss home an awful lot and am becoming very nervous.

Last night, An Khe was shelled with mortar rounds. I hardly knew what was happening. I heard the WHOMP of the explosions, and people around me threw themselves on the ground. A siren wailed and then there was automatic weapons fire outside the barbed wire, close to where I was quartered. The red tracer bullets were flying every which-way.

Six young men were wounded!

AUG
25

Flew to Camp Evans this morning. God, what a mess. The airstrip is considerably smaller and it's nothing but dirt, brown dirt. The heat is overwhelming.

---

1. "Charlie" or "VC" are names given to the Viet Cong by the G.I.s

Only tents and foxholes to live in. There's a beautiful mountain range to the east, but it's peppered with bomb and artillery craters. There are heavy artillery pieces booming constantly.

The farther from Cam Ranh Bay I get, the less conveniences there are. Even water is a problem here. Each man is limited to five gallons a day to bathe, wash clothing, drink, etc. Sometimes I'm told there's no water for a couple of days straight.

AUG
27

Before I went to my unit, there was a preliminary patrol for all newly assigned soldiers. We marched off of Camp Evans last night in full combat gear with a few seasoned veterans. Walked three to four klicks (kilometers) out in defensive fashion, then set up a night observation position on top of a small hill. We dug foxholes completely around the cap of that hill, ate our rations, chose guard hours, and set down mines well out to our respective fronts.

I was with Cowdell, a Utah boy, Crook from Maine, and a sergeant from the mid-west. Talk was limited and light, we only spoke superficially of home.

The next morning, after eating our canned rations, we pulled out and walked down a crooked little trail through the thick green foliage. At a given point, we began to throw hand grenades at suspected enemy positions. I watched the explosions and hated the noise they made. It sounded powerful, more powerful than man himself.

I crouched behind a log, my M-16 at my side. I felt the hard, leafy ground on my face as I lay flat. I held my hands over my helmet, trying to push my head and shoulders into the earth to avoid the deadly shrapnel which was flying through the trees and slicing healthy chunks from them.

Then I was ordered up on the line to throw. My hands were sweaty, my stomach hot. I scrambled forward to cover and pulled a grenade from my flak vest. Others were exploding ahead of us. Crook, the kid from Maine, was on my right flank, ready to discard his just as I was.

I peeked out to my front, held the grenade firmly in my right hand and pulled the pin with my left index finger. I cocked my arm and then BOOM, something happened, I was hit, knocked back. It felt as if an enormous weight landed at the base of my neck and shoulder. As I was being forced back by this tremendous force, I managed either by my own will or by God's to throw my grenade out and over.

Time was racing by, my mind was traveling. What had happened? I lay there screaming, "I'M HIT, I'M BLEEDING," as the concussions sent short, rushing air waves about the area. My chest and neck were saturated with my blood, which felt warm and sticky as I rolled around on the ground, trying to come to my senses.

A medic came and kneeled over me, cutting my shirt away. I began to realize that the explosion came from Crook's position but, lifting my head, I couldn't see him. Everything was taking shape; Crook had mishandled his grenade. How is he? I wondered, as a pressure bandage was forced against my neck and someone put a cigarette in my mouth.

I noticed a sergeant go to the position Crook was at approximately five yards away, shake his head when he looked down, and come running back toward me, assisting in the first aid. I began screaming and swearing at them, inquiring about Crook. They said he would be all right but deep down I knew he wouldn't. I began to cry, cry hard. I could taste the salty tears trying to melt the lump in my throat.

Later, the radioed helicopter set down, pushing and bending all the bushes and grass with the turmoil from its rotor blades. I was treated at Camp Evans, then flown to a Marine base at Quang Tri, six miles from the D.M.Z. They tried to take the shrapnel from my shoulder but could not. I'm being sent to a hospital ship to convalesce.

AUG
30

I'm on the U.S.S. *Repose*, a U.S. Navy hospital ship stationed in the South China Sea, off the coast of Vietnam. Being on the ship is pleasant. I enjoy riding the ocean and looking out to sea. I've been going to movies on board, the food is good. My shoulder is completely numb and my mind is filled with the circumstances concerning my wound. The horror of it all makes me sick.

I feel so much remorse for Crook, and am still really shook as I remember and think of what very well could have been my own fate. Thank you, Lord.

I met a childhood friend of mine aboard who is completely paralyzed. He was hit in the spine with shrapnel. The ship is packed with young men battered and torn by a war we can hardly understand. I hurt, we all do...

SEPT
7

How stupid, I have been put off the ship at Da Nang, far south of my unit's position. I rode the launch in from the ship and made my way to the Da Nang airstrip. I manifested on a cargo fixed-wing flight to Phu Bai and then caught a chopper to Camp Evans and reported to my section for the first time. I met the officers and enlisted men and they all asked about my wound and how I felt. There are a couple of Vietnamese interpreters working here with us.

SEPT
8

My first day with the Civil Affairs & Psychological Operations Section. One of the Vietnamese interpreters was so kind to me. His name is Sergeant So, and he's got the warmest smile I've seen since I arrived in Vietnam.

At approximately 7:15 this evening we were shelled by enemy artillery, just as I was writing a letter. I heard the shells (122-mm rockets) screaming through the air. They sounded as loud as fighter jets when they whistled in. Then there was a distinct crack as they slammed into our company area on Camp Evans. The first one was so close that the concussion almost knocked me from the box I was sitting on. Pieces of metal as big as my fist ripped through the tent.

We all dove outside into our foxholes. My adrenalin was pumping and my stomach burning. I began to pray out loud as they continued to slam in. It lasted nearly five minutes but seemed like five days.

Four dead and fifteen wounded.

I'm full of questions, don't think I'll ever get over it. It was too close for me. I'm confused about a lot of things.

I begin to doubt if I will make it home.

SEPT
18

I've been working at G-5 and getting into the routine of things. One of my jobs is distributing captured enemy rice caches to the people in Phong Dien, a small village not far from here. I can't stand seeing the poverty and disease the Vietnamese people live with. Coming from America so recently, all this is so hard to understand.

My shoulder constantly throbs and I'm conducting my life in a timorous way.

There is a tiny wooden chapel on Camp Evans and I've been making morning Mass daily. I think I've found myself religiously. I'm being forced to.

I think of Jennifer daily. I miss her more than I thought I would. I love her.

I'm getting mail—great.

I don't sleep well at night. Outgoing artillery (ours) makes me jump. I wish it would stop.

It's an eerie feeling being up here away from everything except some crazy Marines—and North Vietnam.

I haven't made any real friends other than Sergeant So.

SEPT 24

We were shelled again this evening at approximately 7:55, just as the sun was going down and that terrible black night time blanket began to cover us. Again they were 122-mm Russian-made artillery shells. I wish I could describe the feeling that grips me when they begin whistling in around me. I know I can't, it's just a personal horror.

It's been raining hard for a week; the monsoon has begun. Everything is wet through and through, including me.

Happiness is dry feet.

The dampness makes my shoulder ache.

SEPT 27

It's a year today since I entered the Army. I can only remember the soft job I had at Fort Detrick before I was ordered to Vietnam. What a change this is.

SEPT 29

Christ! The monsoon is really setting in.

Sergeant So, myself, and two other Vietnamese interpreters have started to build another bunker for our protection. We've been riding the truck to the "sandpoint" (a sandy place to the northeast of Camp Evans where Vietnamese nationals are hired by the U.S. Army to fill sandbags). We need the sandbags for our construction work.

I met a girl today who was working there with the rain driving into her eyes. I gave her a green handkerchief to wipe her face with and she smiled affectionately and stood by my side till we drove off. I'm amazed at the stamina and patience these little workers have.

I must learn to speak Vietnamese.

SEP
30

I got a letter from Julie today. Wow! Was so surprised to hear from her. Julie is the one female I think the most of-but never really got close to. She is Italian-American like myself and I dated her a couple of times during the period when I was working for the New York Telephone Company, had money in my pocket, and owned a British sports car. I had left college and began working. Then I was drafted.

I'm sure that if Julie got to know me truthfully, she would feel as I do. I shall always have these thoughts of a soft and dormant love for her.

I visited the Imperial City of Hue today. We drove down there loaded heavily with ammunition. It's a different Vietnam in the cities.

The commanding officer of G-5 has warned the Section of an enemy artillery barrage which should occur this evening between 7:00 and 8:00 P.M. A P.O.W. was captured outside of Camp Evans and his interrogation report stated that an enemy artillery company was prepared to hit us tonight.

It's 9:15 P.M.-nothing so far.

OCT
1

All quiet last night, false alarm. Very tired now, can hardly keep my eyes open. Today I distributed some more captured rice among the villagers at Phong Dien and visited another 1st Cavalry outpost called Landing Zone Nancy.

OCT
2

Delivered another ¾-ton load of rice to Phong Dien where I spent most of the day. I'm either pitying or falling in love with the Vietnamese people. They have so little in comparison with Americans. I have begun speaking a few phrases of Vietnamese with the help of my little buddy Sergeant So.

A portion of my duties is recording the amount of captured rice denied the North Vietnamese and the Viet Cong. Then the information is passed along to the colonel in charge of my section, who passes it further on to the commanding general of the entire 1st Air Cavalry Division. Everybody but me gets the credit and I do all the work.

My shoulder aches.

OCT
8

I've fallen into a routine, one day seems like the next. I don't even know if its Sunday or Thursday today. There is nothing to distinguish the days; I'm thinking of the smells in Mom's kitchen at home on Sunday afternoons.

I'm having some trouble with the Operations Sergeant in G-5 Section. We don't get on very well.

NEWS FROM THE U.S....

October 11

NASA launches Apollo 7, the first manned Apollo mission, with astronauts Wally Schirra, Donn Eisele and Walter Cunningham aboard. Plans for the mission included the first live television broadcast from orbit and testing the lunar module docking maneuver.

2nd Battalion, 5th Marines engage the NVA in the relief of the besieged Special Forces outpost at Thong Duc. The NVA is driven off after intense hand-to-hand fighting.

October 14

The U. S. Department of Defense announces that the U. S. Army and U. S. Marines will be sending about 24,000 troops back to Vietnam for involuntary second tours.

OCT
9

I've been out at the sandpoint all afternoon and spent the day with Sot, the girl I gave the handkerchief to, trying out my limited knowledge of Vietnamese.

We haven't been hit in a few days.

OCT
10

This dampness and humidity really tell me that I have a piece of metal lodged in my shoulder.

Everything is pretty much routine, I'm even getting used to the 7-pound steel pot helmet I wear.

One of the interpreters went on leave to see his family and I had him pick up some Vietnamese silk for me. He bought it in Saigon and I sent it home.

Not too much mail in the last couple of days because of the monsoon. The heavy rains cause a logistic problem. It becomes difficult getting supply planes through the monsoon weather.

OCT
11

Routine.

OCT
12

A package from home. Will eat well for a couple of days. It makes me feel great.

OCT
13

Got a pillow from Jennifer. It makes me feel real close to her.

OCT
14

Routine, except for the rain. Hasn't let up in four days. Makes things miserable. I take my wet clothes and boots off at night, and in the morning I put them on just as wet.

OCT
15

Don't feel well this evening. Must be a cold or something.
    Still rain.
    K.P. tomorrow.

OCT
16

Have gone to Mass thirty consecutive days!

OCT
28

I heard we are moving. The 1st Air Cavalry is moving down north of Saigon to stop a huge North Vietnamese Army buildup. I'm very scared. We were briefed this morning and we are supposed to be ready for anything. We are going to set up camp in a new area of operations between Saigon and the Cambodian border.

NOV
1

I left Camp Evans today. Huge Air Force C-130s landed at the airstrip. Some of us on jeeps and light trucks drove aboard with supplies and ammunition. We were swallowed up as we drove the vehicles through the giant rear belly hatches.

    After we had strapped the vehicles down and taken off I went up to the flight deck for a smoke. The co-pilot had just left his seat and beckoned to me to come take a look. I did and he sat me down in the cockpit, put the headset on me, and left. I flew at the controls all the way, shooting questions at the pilot a mile a minute. Quite an exciting experience.

    Bombing halted, November 1, 1968. A factor toward peace?

NOV
2

We were hit with mortars at approximately 9:00 P.M. There was a firefight along the perimeter, the Vietcong were shooting into the base camp here at Phouc Vinh.

    This new base camp is smaller than Camp Evans, but it is much better equipped and a hell of a lot more comfortable. There are mess halls here, which means pulling K.P., and all the buildings are permanent. There is no need for tents.

Part of this outpost is an old French compound; that is the portion set aside for the officer's quarters, and I might add that it looks like pretty high living for a combat zone.

NOV
7

I had guard duty last night. I was pacing around the Tactical Operations Center with my M-16 rifle. I thought of home, and of this war, trying to figure out what's right and what's wrong about it all. I jumped and quivered at every tiny noise or flutter-always alert, always. I don't quite understand the mechanics behind a war and its armies; but I'm learning fast.

NOV
14

At approximately 10:45 P.M. we were hit with another barrage of mortar rounds. They began hitting outside the barbed wire pretty close to my position. Then, as Charlie walked them in one by one, they got closer and closer to me until shrapnel pinged through my quarters. Am I to die?

NOV
15

"Doc," the medic in our G-5 unit is becoming quite a friend of mine. He is well educated and well read, but most of all a true and level thinker. I enjoy speaking with him very much. We oftentimes discuss the war and politics. His views on American policy are somewhat harsh, but I respect his ideas and his intellect. He was born in the Fiji Islands, is of Indian descent, and came to study in the United States.

Juarbe, the Puerto Rican kid from the Bronx, feeds another mood of mine. He keeps me alive. This evening before dark we were playing baseball with a ball the Red Cross shipped to us. We were hitting the ball with sticks we broke off of trees, and were constantly getting more sticks as they broke from hitting the ball.

Juarbe is very sensual. He can feel everything. He is a very tender person and lives a good, decent life. He has his own views on the way he should conduct himself and he is terribly closed-minded about it. He loves his wife more than anything in the world. I think he is the type of person who is afraid to try anything new. He is very set in his ways, hates being in Vietnam. He is also very athletic.

Jennifer, Jennifer, I think of you so much. I wish I knew if I was sure. I still rove and gawk at girls. I find the Vietnamese chicks so earthy.

I haven't been theologically conscious to the extreme I was last month. I must get back in the groove.

This confinement and routine is knocking me out.

NOV
16

Outside of camp there is a small river where G.I.s take vehicles to be cleaned. I visited this little wash-point today and saw Vietnamese people selling trinkets, silk, etc. to the G.I.s. There was a multitude of whores wrestling among the reeds with young vulnerable G.I.s for five hundred piasters [2] a piece.

I picked up some odds and ends to send back home for Christmas.

I take it Mom and Dad are very concerned about me. I feel so deeply for them. I received two letters from Dad in the past two days.

I took a darvon—a barbiturate—this evening and became extremely depressed, although later on I had some wine that was sent to one of the boys from home and now I feel absolutely tranquil. I have a wish to do something of intelligence right now. I'm sure the mixture of drugs and alcohol has put me in this mood.

I want to state the philosophy of my favorite Saint—Saint Francis of Assisi—who I think is magnanimous and a symbol of prolific life.

"Lord, make me an instrument of your peace. Where there is hatred, let me sow love. Where there is injury; pardon. Where there is doubt; faith. Where there is despair, hope. When there is darkness; light. Where there is sadness; joy.

"0, divine Master, grant that I may not so much seek to be consoled as to console. To be understood as to understand. To be loved, as to love. For it is in giving that we receive, it is in pardoning that we are pardoned and it is in dying that we are born to eternal life, Amen."

A thought from Daniel Defoe: "But who grudge pain that have their deliverance in view."

---

2.   A piaster is a South Vietnamese monetary note, worth a few cents less than a US. dollar.

And a thought from Mrs. Harold Wilson, "If I can write before I die one line of purest poetry, or crystallize for all to share, a thought unique, a moment rare, within one sentence clear and plain, then I shall not have lived in vain."

NOV
17

I've been flying psychological operations missions in choppers dropping leaflets over battle sites and playing propaganda tapes. Today the ship was shot at and the door gunners opened up on the enemy position, silencing it. Life seems to be very cheap and insignificant in this war. It was electrifying to be shot at.

Today is Sunday. My shoulder is throbbing and the heat is unbearable.

NOV
18

A pal I surfed on Long Island with that summer before I was drafted sent me a surfing magazine. He's been very good to me with mail since I arrived.

Doc picked up WABC on his long band radio. I'm zonked! Heard the time announced as 3.00 P.M. in New York.

Sergeant So returned from leave yesterday. I'm so glad; he is a true and different friend. He had quite a time getting back. He didn't know of our move to this new area of operations.

NOV
19

Started this day with much worry. At the daily briefing by the colonel we were put on alert for a possible ground attack tonight or possibly tomorrow night. It's 7:00 P.M. now and getting dark. The reason is because of the lack of moon during this calendar period. Also, the perimeter was probed last night by the V.C. and the Lights were turned off for security reasons.

I've come to the conclusion that the enemy checks out our barbed wire line, etc. to make it easier for themselves if and when they attack.

I do know if the preceding should occur it would take many, many NVA/VC (North Vietnamese and Viet Cong). Possibly regiment size, and it is not easy for such a large group to move undetected.

No letters today. I wanted to hear from Jennifer so badly.

The pressure doesn't only tax me when we get hit, but thinking of what *might* happen is, I think, my biggest burden in this war. Just as right this moment I realize all too well that I'm a born worrier. My insides will probably age many years during my twelve-month stay in Vietnam.

I'm asking God to watch over my family, not to allow any combat, and to carry me through my duties now, and help me to explore my potential after I return from the military. I also often ask for an end to this bastardly war, and all wars now and to come.

The guys from our hutch went to the whores in the ARVN [3] compound last night. Much to the officers' dismay, it's quite impossible to stop a G.I. from releasing (or relaxing is maybe a better way to put it) himself. The average G.I. will chase a woman's tail for miles. I was quite tempted to join in this escapade, being lonely and away from home and love. But I chose not to. Will record if I do in the future.

Spoke with Doc again this evening.

NOV
20

9:40 P.M. Now! We just got hit with about twenty mortar rounds. This is the closest I've come, and I guess as close as I can get, to being injured without being hurt. Sergeant Richie's hutch received a direct hit and he was wounded in the shoulder. I don't know how bad it is yet.

I'll go out of my mind soon. At 2:15 last night I was awakened by incoming rounds again, over in the helicopter gunship area, not too far away.

I'm Charge of Quarters (C. Q.) [4] tonight and am trembling right now. The rounds land all around me, getting louder and louder. The last one just now was the loudest.

I cannot stand this. I'm so afraid. Good chance to get hit again before the night is over. What can I do?

I feel like running away from this place—Vietnam-altogether. God, please help and protect me and the others concerned. Please!!

---

3.   ARVN means Army Republic of Viet Nam (South Vietnamese soldiers).
4.   Charge of Quarters. or C.Q., means one G.I. on station every evening, whose duty is to guard a unit's office and documents and to take care of any immediate business which may come in during the night

NOV
21

Hit again by mortar rounds at 2:30 in the morning. We will never forget last night. I'm a bundle of nerves. Rockets this time. Sergeant Richie is O.K.; very shook up, though. Saw ARA [5] shooting outside the perimeter tonight. Engaged an enemy sized company. The war is raging here.

I'm too nervous to read or even think.

Got a package from Aunt Janice and from the Veterans of Foreign Wars: Mom and Dad joined. Lots of goodies.

Started an attempt at a mustache. Doubt if it will take. I'm the unhairiest Italian in the world.

Still find time to pray for my family, especially Mom and Dad-and for an end to this war.

Jennifer, I miss you.

Sergeant So is a true friend. I admire the man.

"The United States has wasted its military strength in Vietnam, by applying it gradually."-Richard M. Nixon

---

5.   ARA means Air Rocket Artillery shot from U.S. helicopter gun ships

NEWS FROM THE U.S....

Richard Nixon Elected President: Running on a platform of "law and order". Richard Nixon barely beats out Hubert Humphrey for the presidency.

Nixon takes just 43.4 percent of the popular vote, compared to 42.7 percent for Humphrey.

Third-party candidate George Wallace takes the remaining percentage of votes.

NOV
22

Again, again, again. Will it ever end? Once in broad daylight at 6.00 P.M. (mortars). Then rockets at 2.30 in the morning. I'm half crazed with fear. It's affecting me much worse than the others. I can't eat, don't sleep, can't study anything. I'm not normal under the strain. I'll never be able to write down what I feel now. I can't explain the horror. It's locked up in me, and it hurts. After the rockets came in, I went into the bunker and stayed there all night. God, please come.

Got a beautiful package from Mom and Dad. I love my family so very much. I want to go home to that security now.

Have K.P. on Saturday, November 23.

I'm looking for some way to get out of all this. I'm completely wrecked.

"This only is denied even God: the Power to undo the past."—Agathon

NOV
23

Spent today with much misery and worry. Even during the night I'm sweating.

Was on K.P. today. The new first cook is a bastard. I left early, about 5:00. I just walked out to help those guys build our new bunker complex; I think mainly I was afraid to be far from any protection.

I'm going to go to the priest for some help. I'm toying with my mind, thinking of absurd ways to get out of all this.

Spoke with Doc this evening about my problem. My grave problem! He advised me to see an-army psychiatrist. He said that it was possible for me to have a nervous breakdown. He suggested that I got help. He's so good that way. At first, the word "psychiatrist" shook me up, but maybe one of them can straighten me out. I know I can't go on living like this. Slept in the bunker again tonight.

NOV
24

Today is Sunday. I made an appointment with the chaplain this morning before Mass. During Mass I offered Communion to my parents and family. Also for myself and all in Vietnam, and for an end to the war.

Got a fine letter from Dad this afternoon. It was in answer to the one I wrote him for his birthday.

I know that my problem is worry and it's eating me up. I also know that when the enemy fire starts coming in, everyone is just as scared as I am. But with me, the fright lasts even when it's over. I'm just as scared during the day as I am when we get hit at night. I can't forget about it.

NOV
25

Saw the priest today. We spoke lightly of fate and human life. I feel somewhat better. If I get hit there's nothing I can do about it. There's no way out.

Got hit with rockets at approximately 5:15 PM in broad daylight. Can't wait until this place is cleared up. My knees and elbows scraped and cut again. Ripped my pants diving for cover.

I expect more tonight. According to the pattern I've worked out. We usually get hit in the late afternoon hours, just before the sun sets, and then once again sometime during the night. I watched them shooting along the green line (perimeter).

NOV
26

I'm totally defeated. No defense left in me. I don't know where to turn.

Good letter from Frank and Wayne today. I love my brothers very much. Frank has made me feel good with things he's told me.

I want out of this so badly. Been so very depressed and that's also making me homesick.

The new captain is a great guy to work for. He'll probably take me to Saigon with him at the end of the month. I'd love that.

I think of my brother Jimmy very often. He means a lot to me.

> *"Amen I say to you, all things whatever you ask for in prayer, believe that you shall receive and it shall be done to you."—Mark 11:24.*

> *"When death comes and whispers to me: Thy days are ended. Let me say to him I have lived in love and not in mere time!"*

> *"He will ask: Will thy songs remain? I shall say I know not, but this I know that often when I sang I found my eternity." (Taken from a Mass book.)*

And I say: "We shall laugh again, but we shall never be young again."

NOV
28
Thanksgiving Day

Woke up this morning and heard on the radio that Saigon has joined in the expanded peace talks. I gave thanks. Also thought and meditated for a while on all I have to do and have to be thankful for.

Had Charge of Quarters. Was not digging that too much at all; last time we got hit it was so damn close to me that I bounced off the ground and it made my ears ring.

I feel better. Guess the shock of that night of horror is wearing off. I hope we never get hit again, but I know that's not going to be so.

> *"In all cases war is evil: Who that strikes is not struck in return? Victory and defeat are the same to one who is killed. Defeat is not very much better than death, I think: But he whose side gains victory also surely suffers some loss!"—Maha Bharata*

NOV
29

It's very, very hot. Took a shave and realized how happy doing a little thing like that makes me. Thinking of the day when I'll go home.

It's each man's war as he sees it through his eyes, and reasons through his own mind.

> *"Fear of danger is ten times greater than danger itself."—Defoe*

NOV
30

I got a puppy this afternoon. Doc got him for me. One of the many stray dogs around here had a litter. I named him Forsythe, after the commanding general of the 1st Air Cavalry Division. Major General Forsythe. Thank you, Doc.

DEC
1

Another month has passed. I have two hundred and fifty-nine days left.

Doc left today on R.&R. [6] for Hong Kong. When he returns he is being transferred to another company. My loss, he has given me so much intellectually. I will miss him.

Early this morning there were B-52 bomber strikes about ten miles from here. I swear I thought it was the end of the world. It felt as if the earth would shake loose. Black clouds rose as high as the eye could see.

I'm still extremely worried and often very depressed. I want so bad to make it.

I got a lot of mail today.

I'm still hoping for an early settlement and cease-fire. They say it will be a long time-and it probably will be. Charlie is fighting for position now. He'd love to take Saigon.

DEC
6

More B-52 air strikes.

This morning I was driving for a major in G-5 section, when I almost got shot in the head.

I was driving the jeep with the major on my right when we began to hear firing on the road in front of us, near an M.P. checkpoint. I stopped the jeep and then the firing ceased. The Major ordered me to drive on. As we neared the checkpoint, a machine gun opened up on the vehicle from a tree line on the other side of the checkpoint. The bullets rattled through the metal of the vehicle and the major dove out and crawled to safety in a bunker that the M.P.s were in. Simultaneously, I grabbed my M-16 and rolled out the other side of the jeep, hitting the ground hard.

The major and the M.P.s began firing back, causing a hell of a firefight to take place. Meanwhile, because I had to leave the jeep on the left side, I was away from cover.

Luckily, the ground was slightly higher between myself and the enemy. So I was temporarily out of sight-or so I thought. I knew I couldn't stay there and realized that I had to make it to that bunker and safety, so I lifted my head to try and find the position of the enemy.

Just as I did so, a machine gun burst was fired at me. It was so close that I heard the bullets zing past my head and ears. I knew I was spotted. I felt the heat and tension grab at my stomach. The time was urgent. I had to make my move. Lifting my face from the dirt, I swung my rifle around, jerked the trigger, and

---

6.   Rest & Recuperation.

began spitting bullets back toward the direction of the enemy. I yelled to the bunker for cover and ran to it using every available muscle in my body.

More fire came and kicked up dust around me on my short but long journey to that bunker. I didn't think I could move any faster but I sure did…I sure did! I crawled in behind the sandbags, leaned back, and thanked God.

I felt my heart racing and I could hardly get my breath. It's funny but the whole thing was so exciting; it made me feel so terribly alive and vibrant. I was aware of my young strength and body, my whole being. I can never explain the sensations of war, they are strange, numerous, and various.

In a little while, a helicopter gunship on station buzzed in and began shooting rockets and mini-guns at the position.

Then there was nothing but silence and smoke.

DEC
7

I'm very depressed. All I can think of is the time I have left in Vietnam.

DEC
8

Two hundred and fifty-four days left of my year's tour of duty. I'm almost up to the four month mark.

At 11:05 P.M., five 82-mm Chinese made mortar rounds soared into Phouc Vinh base camp. Negative casualties and damage.

I would like to transfer out of the G-5 section because I detest a majority of the people that I work with. Sergeant Richie is an Army career man. He is unhappy with himself and forces his uneasiness upon everyone around him of lower rank.

Sergeant Baker, who is one stripe under Sergeant Richie and helps run the Psychological Operations Section, also gives us a hard time. But he does it in more of an Army Sergeant's style. Personally, I respect this man, although I would not choose him as a friend.

I wrote Christmas cards last night. The cards were issued to us by our unit. They had a big black and yellow 1st Air Cavalry patch wishing Season's Greetings. Doc and I sent one to President Nixon and one to the President of North Vietnam, Ho Chi Minh.

My puppy, Forsythe, is getting bigger and more playful. He eats as well as I do because I share whatever I get with him.

I wish I could be home for Christmas. It's so special at home this time of year.

DEC
9

An ARVN'S (South Vietnamese Army regulars) trousers hang higher in the front than in the back, while a G.I.s pants hang lower in the front than in the back. Different bellies or asses or something, I guess.

I would like to state my physical ailments:

1. I often have a funny stomach.

2. Feel tired more times than not.

3. My shoulder is always sore.

4. My ears hurt quite often, probably due to the concussions.

5. Eyes sometimes bother me.

I hope I never in my life have to go through two months like November and December of 1968.

DEC
10

There is a young lieutenant in G-5 who gripes me no end. He's a jerk playing soldier boy, and it t tears me apart.

I see too many Vietnamese people whose stomachs are swelled and swelling from starvation, and the poor people who become poorer. I wish I was in charge-I'd do some real good, and help in the right way.

Tonight for the first time since I came to Vietnam, I got high-extra high. I had one beer, than another and another, and in between a couple of shots of Jim's Christmas booze. It was great.

DEC
11

Was promoted to SP/4 [7]today-as of 8 December, 1968. Made me feel good.

Having trouble with my back the last couple of days. It's worse now. It's a funny kind of ache.

No mail for the last couple of days.

---

7.   Specialist 4th Class.

**DEC
12**

I received two Christmas packages from home today. Some wine and food, along with two Christmas gifts. I won't open the presents until Christmas Eve. They also sent me a tape recorder with a tape they had made. I enjoyed that. Miss home very much now. Would love to be there for the holidays. I made a tape and mailed it back to them.

**DEC
13**

Today is Friday the thirteenth.

Lieutenant Vetito, the officer in charge of our broadcasting equipment, sent me to Tay Ninh, another of my unit's base camps. My mission was to deliver a broadcasting set. I flew out early this morning.

When I arrived at Tay Ninh and had finished my military business, I wandered around looking for a meal and a place to rest. I had a couple of hours before my flight back. I wandered into a Philippine compound that is adjacent to the American base camp. The Philippine soldiers were fabulous. They were very kind to me. They fed me rice and chicken and we drank liquor with ice in it from a large pot. They spoke with me. I enjoyed myself.

**DEC
14**

K.P. today.

**DEC
17**

At 6:30 P.M. a few mortar rounds came in. I'm just not sure how it's affecting me this time. I expect more tonight.

Haven't been writing often to anyone. I'm tired of it. Doc is working wonders for my head. I'm getting such an experienced mind. We talk of the WORLD frequently. Doc seems to have visions of personal grandeur. He will be transferred tomorrow. I'm sorry. C.Q. tomorrow night.

Well, after the enemy hit they tried to get into the compound. A lieutenant came around and put us on alert. The lights were out. We had our guns, ammo, and flak jackets. Sergeant Baker came to console us, I think. There was a lot of shooting and hand grenades. They didn't make it through the barbed wire perimeter, though. We are young men, but we act wisely in tight situations.

DEC
21

Received news of Ernie Felece's death, a close friend of my father's. I feel so badly for his family. When I think of Gary, his son, I hurt. I hope it doesn't hurt my Dad too much. I think Mama is stronger that way.

Was picked to go to the Bob Hope Christmas Show today. I really lucked out. The Bob Hope Show is part of an American war. Am flying out to the sprawling military complex at Long Binh, the headquarters of the US. Army in Vietnam.

DEC
22

Arrived at Long Binh about 8:00 A.M. Nice place. Sure would like to be stationed there. Stateside clubs, snack bars, American girls! Wow what a groove!

The Bob Hope Show was a very colorful production and each of the girls he brought with him from the States was a scantily-clad knockout. At the end of the Show, when we all sang "Silent Night" my eyes filled with tears.

Tomorrow I will fly back to my unit at Phouc Vinh.

DEC
25

I'm back and smothered over by the same old Army routine.

It's Christmas and I am sad because I can feel no peace in the world.

DEC
27

I met a Vietnamese girl today. She works in the P.X. here in Phouc Vinh. I'm really attracted to her. It's so good to feel like a person again instead of a grubby dirty unshaven G.I.

It's basic to me to have normal interactions with women. I don't feel complete without this.

DEC
29

Oh, what a day! Thuy Tien is her name. I have flipped over this girl. She is so graceful and beautiful and she is a good person. I hate this war for keeping me from her every minute.

We communicate through letters, using Sergeant So as our interpreter. I'm pushing hard now to speak Vietnamese. I study every spare minute I can get.

I've been doing some civil affairs work at the Civilian Personnel Office. I'm away from the officers and sergeants all day. Great. I don't have to take any crap from them. There is also this Vietnamese girl named Van who works there and this makes for a pleasant atmosphere.

At 8:10 this evening, I was reminded suddenly and promptly that indeed there is a heavy war going on. We were hit hard with better than forty rounds of artillery. There was a mixed bag of incoming rounds including 107-millimeter rockets, 82-mm mortar fire, and something brand new to me, recoilless rifle fire. A recoilless rifle is an artillery piece, which is extremely accurate because of its superior sighting device. We were hit four times in two hours. More blood, more fright, more death.

DEC
31
1968
New Year's Eve

At 9:00 P.M. one single round came in. I'm sure that the goddamn enemy didn't fire it to cause damage or injury but as more of a harassing measure because it's New Year's Eve and they know there is celebrating and gaiety going on. Now everyone is just moping around, thinking of home and being very cautious.

JAN
1
1969

New Year's Day was just like any other. Christmas was much the same.

I gave Tien another letter today and received one from her. But I really flubbed up. I embarrassed her an awful lot. I handed her the letter on the street and that was a grave mistake. According to Vietnamese custom, it is forbidden to display any emotion publicly between man and woman. It's wrong even to call out a girl's name in a public place. But being typically middle-class American, it's hard for me to understand such strict convention.

Jennifer isn't writing like she used to; she seems to have lost comprehension. Her letters were so strong and understanding up until now.

JAN
2

I'm starting to realize how much friendship means in a situation such as this. I couldn't make it alone. Each of my buddies helps me in a different way. There is Doc who brings out the comprehension and capacity in me, and of course Sergeant So who has given me so much understanding of and compassion for a foreign culture. Juarbe, the Puerto Rican kid, helps in warding off my liberal ideas.

Two other G.I.s are close to me, too. One of them is Alabama. He is good-hearted and very southern in his ways. He will bend over backwards to help someone. He is extremely talkative and friendly. Alabama has average intelligence and keen wits. I like him a lot and am sure that the girl he marries will be a very lucky person.

Al is also the biggest wheeler-dealer I have ever seen. It's so funny to see him in action. He knows every single G.I. and officer on this base camp and they all know him. He is constantly trading, selling, and borrowing things. No matter what is needed, Alabama can get it.

The other of my pals is Blanchard. He's a regular Joe in every sense-a hell of a nice guy. Blanchard comes from a broken home and was brought up on the streets of Jersey City. I'm sure that if he was steered in the right direction he would have made good intellectually. He quit high school, married early, and has a police record, but he is still quite a guy. He reminds me of my Dad sometimes. He doesn't worry about anything and always keeps a cool head. I like him.

JAN
3

Oh! Thuy Tien-I think of you constantly. I am beginning to fancy myself marrying her, bringing her home, and living a nice quiet life. But my intellectually starved mind tells me to be selfish and do what I have to do for myself and to myself.

MYSELF: "I have miles to go and promises to keep."

Doc visited me tonight. How much I miss talking to him. He has opened me up so much. The more I think, the more it hurts.

I'm an angry young man.

I don't write down my thoughts of the other personnel in G-5 because they aren't worth my bother, with the exception of Shep perhaps.

NEWS FROM THE U.S....

January 10

After 147 years, the last issue of the *Saturday Evening Post* is published

January 12

Super Bowl III: One of the biggest upsets in American sports history. The American Football League (AFL) champion New York Jets defeat the National Football League (NFL) champion Baltimore Colts in Miami, Fla,16–7, in the first Super Bowl victory for the AFL.
After boldly guaranteeing a victory prior to the game, Jets controversial quarterback Joe Namath (Super Bowl's Most Valuable Player) completed 17 out of 28 passes for 206 yards.

January 30

The Beatles' gave their last public performance in an impromptu concert on the roof of Apple Records.

JAN
6

I've got the willies tonight. I'm scared. I'm so afraid of dying. I'm also afraid for my family. I know they are going through hell. I HATE this war so damn much. I hate it more than the word hate can express.

Tomorrow is Tien's birthday.

Tien will be nineteen years old on January 7,1969. She is a thin girl with long straight jet-black hair. She wears bangs. She must be around 5'3" and has a slightly curved back. A good thing according to an old Chinese proverb.

Her face is round and has color. She has a light complexion for a Vietnamese girl.

A nice smile she wears! But it is interrupted by a gold-capped tooth. I think she looks better in dark colors. I could make her look beautiful.

She is intelligent, sharp, and has a good memory. I'm sure she is quite sincere.

Tien possesses that rare quality of femininity, which makes me secretly desire a woman. I can tell just by looking at her that she would make an excellent wife, good homemaker, mother, etc. This is the type of girl I want to marry someday. I have seen this quality only twice before. My Mom has it and Julie has it. I know this is why I was so sure with Julie. I call her "my Italian Heart-throb."

Tien's body is not one that deserves wolf whistles. As I said before she is thin. She is small-breasted and small hipped. I appreciate small girls, though. I'm sure that if I were to marry her I would go crazy making love to her. I can see it in her face that she'd make her husband happy and know very well how to take care of him.

Jennifer in comparison is fun, immature, very American, and I think sometimes selfish. She is clean, has beautiful hair and teeth. I'd put her intellectual level on a par with mine. We both have ample ability but should work harder at things than we do. She comes from a comfortable family which I have certain thoughts about) and has pretty much had whatever she wanted. She dresses nice, sometimes too young though.

Jennifer has a nice body, and truthfully I desire her right now. I'm certain that she loves sex. Although I've never slept with her, our frequent petting has shown me that she has great desire and she will probably remain that way even when she grows old.

I love Jennifer and have thought of marrying her. I know that a marriage to Jennifer would be fun and happiness in the beginning. I can picture us traveling, engaging in sports, night-lifing. I can see a groovy apartment and a new sports car. The whole bit! But after that, I don't know. I don't think she would be a good homemaker. I don't think she would be happy settled down with a bunch of kids. I don't think she could take care of a baby well. That's another one of those hidden treasures I can see in a girl.

I guess I'm not sure of anything. I'm not very consistent at all.

For myself-l would like to finish school and become an English teacher. I'm sure I would be happy teaching high school. I only hope and pray that I can hack three more years of school.

I want so many things. I want an education, I want to know the world I live in. I want to have money enough to live well.

I want to meet interesting people. I want a peaceful earth.

I want a good wife someday, a few children, and an excellent home.

I want to live!, and I want to see God when my time comes.

Dominick, it's your life!!

JAN
8

Yesterday Tien did not have a reply for the letter I gave her. I was kind of shook. But today she gave me a letter with a picture of herself. Her letters are suggestive but cautious. I think she is afraid to let herself become emotionally involved with me. I don't like it. I think I could be in love with her. I hurt…

I contacted Marc yesterday by mail. We have decided to take an R. & R. to Australia together in the last week of April.

I've been talking with Van, the Vietnamese girl, at the C.P.O. (Civilian Personnel Office). She's good and has much to be desired. I admire her hands so damn much. I watch her write and scratch her cheek with her index finger and I can see a world of femininity.

JAN
10

Gave Tien a letter, good day for us. Linda, an old girl friend of mine, is writing to me everyday. She's a nice girl, and I think she is possibly looking for someone.

Got a letter from Marc; he explained his first acid trip. He's out to experience everything. Even L.S.D. Quiet, sensual Marc.

JAN
14

Been in a bad mood for the last three days. Haven't gone to see Tien since Sunday. I'm bugged by her shyness. She is very Vietnamese in her ways. I'm tired and I want to go home.

I'm identifying with the poems of Rod McKuen that Jennifer sent me for Christmas.

JAN
15

Spent today inoculating pigs and cows with the veterinarian. It was my duty to hold the animal while the vet gave the shots. It was a good deed for the people of Vietnam and myself too. I had fun and was off the compound all day. I really enjoyed myself. Ate lunch in town with the vet. I saw a bar girl who made my blood boil. Next chance I get with a half-decent looker I'm taking. I'm horny as hell.

Alabama is going on PSYOPS [8] combat assault tomorrow. Good luck, my friend. Come back safe.

No time for Tien today.

JAN
16

Went to see Tien this morning and she gave me two letters. In both letters she told me how happy I've made her, and how she hates living in constant war. I'm so lonesome for a girl who is different and not false. I'm attracted to girls who have a different quality than I, even though they have another background.

I'm so confused about what I want out of life and how to get it. Sometimes I say to myself:

"If I'm captured, I want to see Ho Chi Minh."

"If I'm killed, I want to see God."

JAN
22

A fine day. Spent much of it in Phouc Vinh. I ate sugar cane and mangos. I drank Vietnamese beer and ate Vietnamese food. I made friends with little children and

---

8.   PSYOPS, Psychological Operations.

I smiled at old men and women and they smiled back. I feel so young and full of life and kindness.

I also got a l look at Tien's family today. I'm impressed. We haven't been hit in approximately three weeks. Expect it any day.

Got a card from *Julie* this afternoon…

Linda is still writing. I'm going to make it a point to see her when I get home.

JAN
25

All is as well as can be expected. I picked up a letter from Tien yesterday. I was hoping for it to be more romantic. It's becoming hard for me to face her. One thing that surprised me was that yesterday she handed me the letter without worrying that anyone would see her giving it to me. Maybe this is a good sign!

I just finished conversing with Doc and, as always, we spoke of this world and the war. I'll never be able to repay him for his influence on me.

Van is a woman, she's lovely and feminine, and I'd love to sleep with her. I adore her and enjoy being close to her. I think she is secretly in love with me or else likes me an awful lot.

I received a letter from Marc today and it was great. We'll most probably be going to Australia together.

I worry about Dad's heart very much. He is only 43 but he has a serious heart condition. I am terribly worried for him. The boys tell me that Mom and Dad are fine and I can't explain how happy and contented this makes me. I want my Mom and Dad to always be together in mind, spirit, sincerity, and love. I love them both.

Jennifer, I hardly think of you-lately that is. I don't know, maybe it's not real love with us but just an infatuation.

She hardly knows my thoughts although I have tried to put them down on paper to her.

Tet, the Vietnamese New Year, is coming up and everybody is kind of getting ready for it. Busying themselves building bunkers, etc. We all expect to catch hell for Tet and frankly I wouldn't be surprised if we did. The 1st Air Cavalry hauled in the highest ammo and arms cache of the war. This makes me feel somewhat sure that the VC/NVA have already set something up for Saigon during Tet. It's possible for all hell to break loose around here in the very near future.

Two hundred and four days left.

JAN
26

Today, although I didn't go to see Tien at the P.X., I watched her walk by when she got off from work. I love everything about her. The way she looks, talks, everything.

She keeps herself well and clean. At 5:00 P.M. I went to Mass in Phouc Vinh- a Vietnamese Mass. It was a high mass and it was beautiful. It reminded me of Saint Paul's, a Catholic school & church I attended in Manhattan as a boy. The men sit on one side and the women on the other with the children toward the front. The women sing and the men answer. Very elaborate and spiritual.

The high point for me was when I saw Tien come into church. She didn't know I was there, but I saw her. She looked so real and beautiful to me. I'll never forget how she struck me at the time, dressed in the traditional Ao Dao, or costume of Vietnamese women. It was a pale blue and she had white silk slacks on underneath. I loved her just then; l was sure of it. I love without knowing too very much about her. *Why?* I wish I was done with school and ready to settle down at times such as this.

While I was on C.Q. tonight, I wrote to Mom and Dad about how I feel towards Tien. I asked them exactly what I ask myself: How can *a man be sure that this is the* woman for *him?* I tried to be amusing in my letter because the whole thing *is* kind of amusing. I hope I don't cause any grave concern or worry to them, and I am debating with myself about whether or not I was right in consulting them. I am so inconsistent.

K.P. tomorrow.

Haven't been into any books for a while. I must start reading again.

I want to cry when I think that someday my parents will be fifty, then sixty, and even older.

JAN
29

Tien wasn't at work today. I saw her in town though, but I didn't stop in to see her because there were other G.I.s in the laundry. She is so very near to me and yet so far away.

I get tee'd off when I see her with someone else. I have a letter for her...

Started to read a book.

Wrote to Julie; it's so unspoken between us.

Jennifer...well, I don't know.

Haven't been hit for over a month now. What will Tet bring? What will Nixon bring?

Got a package from home. Dad sent a bottle of scotch. Thank you, Pop. Also got some dog food from home for Forsythe. They are great people and each is very loved by me.

Van is off to Bien Hoa for a few days. I miss her at work.

I think Sergeant So is taking more of an interest in me than usual. He seems to understand what I'm striving for.

Mail is screwed up for some odd military reason.

I'm beginning to get short…

One hundred and ninety-nine days to do…

This may very well be the calm before the storm!

FEB
2

2:00 P.M. Love is just as painful as war, except that it has a different kind of hurt.

Tien's letter to me today expressed her feelings; that she doesn't want to become emotionally involved, and that she wants to regard me as a friend, and console me while I am away from my home and family. Whether these are her true feelings or not, I'm not sure. But I am deeply hurt. Without having her to look up to me, it will be hard. I will no longer have reason to put on fresh fatigues, shave my face, and shine my boots. She made every day in this short forty days something to look forward to. A reason to wake up in the morning.

I don't know what to do now or how to act. I do not want to forget about Tien. Maybe I can't, but I love her even more for her sensible thoughts. She reminds me so much of Julie now; they think alike. I think Tien is afraid to let herself love me because she thinks that I will go home in six months and forget about her. To leave her with the memory of us. She says she is thinking of the future.

But I too am thinking of the future and I have thought of bringing her home. What stops me is the fact that I have so much to do. "I have miles to go and promises to keep."

5:45 P.M. I'm drunk and depressed but mostly I'm hurt because I feel as if I've lost. I feel self-conscious. Why can't I have what I want? Why should it end so soon?

6:45 P.M. What's a woman for? What are they after? I'm sure that I give a girl much more praise than many other men do. Is a woman's job not to worship a man? And a man's job not to worship a woman? If I offer a female myself, why does she insist on doubting? Are we not meant to care for and love each other?

Our countries are holding Tien and myself apart. She is everything I want and more.

Orientals are the most beautiful women I have come in contact with.

The trouble with me is that I have begun to see myself in everyone who is troubled.

FEB
4

K.P., officer's mess…another day gone by.

Finished my book. It was good entertainment reading. I must keep reading now.

I gave Tien a letter yesterday in English telling her I didn't care how she felt—that it couldn't change my love for her.

FEB
5

Goodbye, Hoang Thuy Tien.

American women are sensuous only until you marry them; then they make love as though all the window shades were up. When American women change, they go overnight from 20 to 80. I read that somewhere.

FEB
8

Phouc Vinh was put "on limits" for G.I.s today. All the G.I.s are on Cloud 9. I want to get into town as much as possible.

I've been neglecting everything; my praying, my reading, and sometimes my thinking. It hasn't been as broad as in the last couple of weeks. I've slowed down on writing also. My puppy Forsythe left or was stolen or something. At any rate, he is gone and I miss him. I hope to find him soon.

FEB
9

Today, for the first time in my life, I paid to sleep with a whore. Blanchard and I got passes to go to town and we went in this afternoon. We walked around quite a bit, stopping in a laundry now and then for a beer. Vietnamese laundries in Phouc Vinh usually are also saloons. I got a good charge on. I was quite high.

At any rate, on our way back to the base we got hooked up with this kid who snuck up past the M.P.s and in a back alley and backyard to the rear of this bar. Feeling the liquor I was quick to indulge. I can honestly say now that it wasn't worth the time or the money. Sex in its simplest form is nothing more than a rushed sensation to me. I'm quite sure that some emotion must be felt for any kind of real pleasure.

This evening I'm awfully exhausted. Most likely from the day I had.

I saw Tien and I hurt immediately. If I don't see her, I'm o.k., but as soon as I do my fire is lit again. I just don't know why she has done this or what her thoughts really are. I have my doubts. Anyway I feel defeated and lost, and that hurts more than anything else.

Got a lot of mail today, including another tape. I'm so angry that I cannot make another tape to send home because my microphone is out.

FEB
12

Today my job was to guard nine North Vietnamese prisoners. I shouldn't call them prisoners because they weren't captured, they surrendered. I enjoyed my stay with them. Most were actually very likable. I had to stay overnight to guard them, at the interrogation point, and during this time we became quite good friends. When we parted they all gave me little notes to be translated. They said things like "long life" and "many happy children", etc. How can I call these men my enemies?

Sergeant So works side by side with the G-5 officers, interpreting and translating military stuff to the prisoners. To my surprise, he displays much compassion in his role as a middleman.

FEB
15

My puppy has been missing for a couple of days, and today I found out that the company commander of the 545th M.P. Brigade shot him to death. Yesterday, when I learned this, I was truly and deeply hurt because I had a growing love for that puppy. I'm angry at the bastard that killed him.

I filed a complaint at the I.G. [9] today, and went to get a look at the bum that shot Forsythe.

He was a stock type army man, with a square chin and he wore his helmet down shading his eyes. He spoke with a southern accent. On my initial encounter with him, I began the conversation by calling him a "goddam bum" and asked if he would like to shoot me, too. He barked back at me, calling me to attention and ordered me to stop my insubordination. After chewing me out, he dismissed me.

I'm sure he realized how angry I was, and I'm also sure that he realized I was carrying a rifle, just as big and as lethal as the rifle he had. With this at hand, I was able to escape further military discipline. (There has been at least one incident here on base where a sergeant was wounded in his sleep by a person or persons unknown.)

I'm thinking of writing the President about this incident.

I visited a Buddhist Temple today. I wasn't very impressed.

The guys down at the other end of the hutch were drunk last night and started picking on Alabama. At 3:15 in the morning they woke him up and started horsing around, but Blanchard came to his rescue. The powder is there for a big fight now. All we need is the spark.

Tet is in the air and seeing all these little people happy makes me happy. The celebrating starts tomorrow night and lasts for three days and nights.

Van invited me to her house tomorrow and truthfully I'm dying to go. If they screw up my pass, I'll scream.

I got Tet cards for Van and Thuy Tien.

I heard today that Tien is very sick and has been for the past couple of days. I will bring her card to the laundry tomorrow. Whenever I see her, I love her.

Mom and Dad answered my letter and seemed a little concerned about the situation, but they sent me great advice about love relationships, and man's and woman's place in the world. It's funny but I expected to get Mom's ideas out of Dad and vice versa.

Spent the afternoon with Doc today. He has very little time left in Viet Nam.

Got a bunch of great pictures from home. I miss them all so much. I can get along alone now though, but I will miss them always.

One hundred and eighty-one days to go…

Blanchard, Juarbe, Alabama, and myself are the four musketeers.

---

9.   Inspector General.

FEB
16

My sister Angela sent another letter today. She is an amazing young girl. Bunny (our nickname for her) is the youngest of our family, and she is Daddy's little girl. She came to my parents after four boys and is kind of the silent member of our family. We boys huskily overpower her at home, and always tease her. She never says much, but always seems to know what is going on. I miss teasing her. I really love my sister Bunny.

FEB
18

I had a pass last Sunday and went into town to visit Van at her home. Her house is much better than other VN homes.

Van asked to borrow fifty dollars from me. I lost a lot of feeling for her because she borrowed money from me. I'm afraid she may try to use me. So many Vietnamese girls do use naive G.I.s.

Last night I got sick. Woke up about 2:00 P.M. with cramps. I threw up and had the runs. I was a bit delirious today. Had a bunch of weird dreams. I spent the day in bed.

A quiet tet, to my surprise.

FEB
20

Tonight and last night we have been on partial alert because of a possible ground attack. I know something bad is in the air. I can feel it. Scared.

FEB
23
Sunday

It has started! The long awaited offensive has most probably begun. There were mortar and rocket attacks on over a hundred cities and military installations. Saigon was hit twice, once early this morning and once at 6:25 P.M. this evening.

Every L.Z. (landing zone) and outpost of the 1st Cavalry was hit hard last night. Everyone Including Phouc Vinh. We caught a mixed bag of fifty-three 107-mm rockets and mortars. I was on C.Q. last night and, to tell the truth, I've been feeling pretty secure lately, even on C.Q. because we haven't been hit in about two weeks.

Anyway, about 3:15 A.M., I was awakened by the first round of the first barrage, which hit the general's drivers' hutch directly. Both drivers were killed. I scrambled for the bunker and I had just got into the entrance when another one hit in front of the officer's latrine, approximately one hundred feet away from me. After that they just rained in all around the area, kicking up dust and shrapnel. I thought about dying then. I was alone in the bunker praying out loud, thinking, and scared as hell.

After the first barrage, I conjured up enough guts to run in and get my clothes and cigarettes and then went back into the bunker to get dressed. They were still coming in. When it quieted down some, I ran over to the G-4 bunker just so I could be with someone-anyone. People were in there and I felt somewhat relieved. At 4:15, the 107s started whistling in again and landed all around the compound. It happened again at 6:15 when I thought for sure it was all over because it was beginning to get light.

Fifty-three rounds in all.

I heard funny clicks before each impact. Two clicks and then the explosion. That was a new sound…

My ears are the most important part of my body, I think, in this time of war.

Don't know if we'll get hit again tonight, but I'm feeling lousy again. This is a time to pray and think. I got a good tape from home. I wish I were there with them so much.

Ben Hoa received a ground attack and was shelled. Even Cam Rahn Bay was hit…

I finished reading *The Catcher in the Rye* by J. D. Salinger.

> *"The mark of an immature man is that he wants to die nobly for a cause, while the mark of a mature man is that he wants to live humbly for one."—Sergeant So.*

FEB 25

I've been thinking about dying. If a Red rocket or mortar gets me, there's nothing I can do. The enemy has broken down my will somewhat. Nine more prisoners came in today. I didn't choose to be at all friendly. Most probably because of Sunday morning's attack. Those rounds came so close they nearly had me. I will never ever forget that Sunday morning. I guess I can consider myself a seasoned combat soldier after nineteen standoff attacks by enemy artillery and my brief encounter under automatic machine gun fire.

Sometimes I wish I would get hit again just so I could get the hell out of here.

Tonight, when the B-52s flew over and I heard their huge bombs detonating, I didn't feel sorry for the enemy. I was glad he was getting hit!

I've hid myself like a dog the past couple of days, sleeping in the bunker (that crummy hole). I really dread C.Q. and K.P.

Haven't seen Tien in almost three weeks. She has been very sick. I'm told she will be back at work in a day or two.

I had to guard some more prisoners in a South Vietnamese compound. While I was there I saw many very small naked children. They were so dirty. The elders were busying themselves with feeding the kids, some were moping around smoking. Some were just sitting or standing on the steps of that awfully filthy shelter they have. Inside there are bare rooms-absolutely bare, not a trace of furniture except for a lone bench or hammock. They were eating rice out of dirty mess kits, most of which were bent out of shape.

One young boy had a bandage wrapped completely around his waist. Three or four women were limping on bandaged feet. One of them couldn't walk at all. This is the result of Communist shellings the Sunday before. Many of these innocent, poverty-stricken people were wounded.

It's odd to see so many three, four, and five year old boys and girls carrying their one and two year old brothers and sisters. Amazingly enough, they go about their task without a frown or gripe, and they do it with great agility.

I have seen so much.

FEB
26

Approximately fifteen minutes ago at 8:55 P.M. a barrage of mortars came in. This was the twentieth time I've been under artillery fire. I can be sure of more tonight. Possibly there will be a ground attack. I hope and pray not, though.

9:30 P.M. I just got done watching a real bang-up show. I think we might have located and hit the mortar team, because two cobra gun ships gave it all they had for about a half-hour. In Vietnam there is nothing like a chopper to lift a guy's faith and reassure him a bit. We may be scared, but we're tough.

FEB
27

Between the humidity and getting hit it seems that everyone is on edge. We're all irritable.

This afternoon, Alabama and I got passes to go to town, and we slept with whores. The girl I got was Chinese and very womanly. I enjoyed her very much, and she satisfied me. The room we were in was pleasant and the time I spent just talking and horsing around with her and Alabama was enjoyable. I feel so complete. Made tapes to send home...

FEB
28

Well, another month gone and another month closer to home. We've started to build a bunker inside the hutch; otherwise, not too much to say.

I'm still thinking of the good time I had with that Chinese girl yesterday.

MAR
4

At 10:30 this morning a few mortar rounds came in and hit around the airstrip.

I have the C.Q. tonight and I'm sweating it out. I hope we don't get hit during the day anymore. I hope we don't get hit at all anymore.

Our bunker is coming along nicely.

First time we were hit during the late morning hours.

MAR
5

Got a tape from home today and Mom and Dad said they haven't heard from me in two weeks and they sounded awfully worried. I made two return tapes.

Slept in the bunker at the office on C.Q. last night. I'm scared tonight. I think I may die.

Linda is still writing.

MAR
6

At 3:30 this morning, a 107-mm rocket hit just a couple of feet out in front of the hutch. It hit the 3/4-ton truck and completely destroyed it. The concussion rocked me right out of my bed. The round hit no more than twenty feet from me and no more than five feet from Alabama and Sergeant So. If it had been five feet closer, we all would have died. The two right wheels of the truck were in the ditch alongside the hutch. The round just missed the roof. That, too, would have been sure death.

Another round hit in the road about one hundred feet in front of G-4; another one in the back of G-4. The rest of the thirty some rounds peppered HHC. Two G.I.s from G-4 were wounded in the legs. This is even closer than the last time on February 23.

I know there is a God. I'm sure of it. I started to give some thought to the popular G.I. theory of fate: when it's your time to go, you'll go. Maybe it's not my time to go. I never put much stock in that thought before, but I do now. I have somewhat prepared myself for death because of the extremely close calls I have had during the past ten days. What can I do? It's hell, it stinks. Just think of it. I might DIE!

Again, at approximately 6:15 P.M., a few more rockets came in. One hit the P.X. (again) and blew the whole side out of the building.

This was my first experience with delayed fuses,[10] no bunker, hole, etc. is secure if it takes a direct hit with a delayed fuse.

This afternoon I went to town with Sergeant Sharpe and I saw Wanh (the girl I slept with last week). To make a long story short I slept with her this time for free. She really knows how. I can probably sleep with her every time I get to town. I realize that I'm sinning, but then again I must live for right now because of my present situation.

Saigon got hit again. Many innocent civilians are getting wounded. What Nixon will do remains to be seen. Maybe this new offensive will have some influence in Paris...?

P.S. Thank You, God. Thank You. I also want to say that all night March 5th I had a funny feeling, like something was going to happen. It's strange but I really knew. I'm not sure what this feeling is. Is it a premonition? Or is it possibly God calling me, and trying to tell me that the Viet Cong and/or North Vietnamese are setting up artillery shells and aiming them at me? It's not the kind of feeling I can easily speak of to someone. It's inside of me, and I know it's there.

But I don't understand it.

---

10. Delayed Fuse-an artillery round that is timed to detonate seconds after impact, allowing it to bury its warhead into the target before exploding.

MAR
11

Some mortar rounds came in early this evening. They were respectfully away from my position. I think I'm sort of becoming used to being shelled with artillery because I'm not in the bad way I was last November.

Naturally I always worry, though, and it's a constant pressure on me. When they come close, I'm crazed with fear. I've adopted a kind of philosophy toward it, however. Actually what I think I do is to make it plain and logical in my mind and set up a personal kind of defense, but I realize this too will be upset as soon as I have another close call.

A prisoner of war was picked up last night snooping around the perimeter. During his interrogation he stated that our camp was supposed to receive a heavy attack in the near future.

I applied for a Rest and Recuperation (R&R) to Australia at the end of March, but I was turned down because Australia is a very popular spot for vacationing G.I.s and the infantrymen have first priority, justly so.

Jennifer, my U.S. of A. girl friend sent me some pictures of herself. She looks good and I have somewhat renewed my feelings toward her. I'm so confused about women.

I picked up a book by Hemingway titled *The Sun Also Rises*. I haven't been able to grasp everything in the book, but I see that Hemingway writes in a very realistic style. When I put the book down, I and everything around me seems so truthful.

I saw Tien today and my fire was lit again. I must control myself. She has been sick with hepatitis for the past month.

I'm trying to get into town to sleep with Wanh, that Chinese girl.

It's 8:45 P.M. now and I just had to scramble for cover because we were hit with some rockets. I'm scared because they sounded heavy-like 122-mm rockets. I'm going to stop writing and make myself as secure as possible.

MAR
13

I went into Phouc Vinh today. I bought some marijuana and I slept with Wanh before returning to camp. I won't go back to her again because I feel she has some kind of an angle. It's strange, but I think I can sense it through our language barrier and different thinking minds. I've got enough to worry about.

Away and out of the sight of the others, I smoked three joints of "grass" this evening. I want to experiment. I realize what I'm doing is harmless because I'm in complete control of myself and couldn't get carried away. Anyhow, I want to learn. I became relaxed and a little loose, nothing too drastic, no real big flip out.

Marijuana is readily and very easily obtainable to every G.I. in Vietnam. This is fact. For two dollars one can buy a very cleverly concealed bulk of "grass." It is packaged in the exact same manner as a pack of American cigarettes, with name brands, filters, and cellophane sealing. Damn smart; someone is making big money. Many soldiers depend on it the way I need clean water.

MAR
14

When I offend myself, then I also offend God.

MAR
19

Today I was flying psychological operations missions in a chopper, as I do many days. Flying is exciting but I wish it were under more pleasurable circumstances.

The enemy offensive is still in full swing.

I've finished that book by Hemingway.

MAR
21

I want women to give themselves without defenses. To sink and become submerged in me.

What goal can a women conceive except happiness? She should assume her responsibility and set off toward her goal. Happiness—that and nothing else.

MAR
22

I've got to get to Europe sometime in the near future. I've given the Peace Corps some thought also.

Here are a couple of quotes from Hemingway, which I found enjoyable.

"It was like certain dinners I remember from the war. There was much wine, an ignored tension, and a feeling of things to come that you could not prevent happening....

"After supper we went upstairs and smoked and read in bed to keep warm. Once during the night I awoke and heard the wind blowing. It felt good to be warm and in bed."

Both of these are worth praise because they set up a mood and feeling in a credible sense.

MAR 23

I was in town this afternoon and I met a clean and bright-eyed girl named Hoa. She is not the best looking girl in the world but she seems to be a fine person. Talking to her, I felt all the hardship and turmoil a young, ambitious person in Vietnam faces. She explained that someday she would like to go to medical school. She is trapped by the war and all its dirt. Her chances are impossible. I want to see her regularly.

MAR 25

The first volley of rockets rained in all around us, detonated on impact, and exploded with an ear-piercing crack and a flash bright enough to light up an entire night. As I scrambled and scratched for the best possible protection, I watched the others. I noticed an urgent expression on each of my friends' faces who had just been awaked at 3 A.M. by hostile enemy fire. Our moods and needs are exact at these times.

No one could sleep, everyone was quiet, and cigarette ends became brighter as we passed them around in the still dark and damp blackness of the Vietnam night.

We began to feel easier about 6 A.M. when the sky started to change from black to gray. But suddenly we heard the familiar whining whistle of incoming artillery. I heard them pepper the whole area. I lay flat with my hands pressing my helmet as far over my head as I could get it. The rounds were extremely close. One five foot, fifty pound 107-mm rocket (most likely manufactured in Russia) hit the tin roof of a small building directly across the small dirt road. Four men that I knew were killed eight others were severely wounded. There was a huge hole ripped through the roof.

Everybody and everything in that small building was hit with shrapnel. Blood and flesh lay in small disgusting pools on the ground. I noticed a charred, smoldering mattress that was sizzling the remains of an American's young body. I thought then of his folks back home. I asked God *why?* Then I cursed this no good bastardly war.

MAR
26

They started shelling us again at about 11:45 P.M. and hit us hard four times. It lasted until just before dawn. Something is up, they are hurting us badly. Another sleepless night. Everyone is so scared. I hope this offensive ends soon. Thinking of home is all that keeps me going.

MAR
27

Some rockets came in at approximately 6:50 P.M.; they started shelling us early this evening. What is in store for the rest of the night is pretty obvious.

I got a package from home containing lots of goodies and a tape. It's swell to hear the voices of the folks back home.

MAR
28

When I drink, I often go inside myself to groove on a place that is softened by the music and the accompanying words.

MAR
30

It is Palm Sunday. As the Mass was being conducted, it was interrupted by the screeching and detonating of rockets being shot into the base camp. They landed over by the airstrip. I can't believe this happening during daylight hours on Palm Sunday; there is no escape from it. It is a constant fear that lives in me just as sure as *I* live. It's part of my life here.

I will be recalling Christ's life and teachings during this holy week of nineteen hundred and sixty-nine. It only boosts my stand on how wrong this war is.

The everyday routine of the Army and the constant shelling have made me very depressed.

MAR
31

Another month gone by.

APR
1

Early this morning another salvo of enemy artillery unpleasantly wailed over my head and smashed the pre-dawn stillness with bright flares and concussions. it wounded and maimed young American men.

I oftentimes wonder if the people back home really know what we are going through.

APR
2

We are supposed to get hit hard this evening, according to Army Intelligence. We have been alerted to stay in bunkers. That is where I am now, my back against the damp, cool earth. I am writing by candlelight. I'm talking to God right now as I look up and watch the reflections dance on the sandbag ceiling.

A patrol which left from here this morning found an obviously placed rocket, set up for firing, with a note attached. Printed in English the note read: "How do you like this one, First Air Cavalry Division?"

I'm beginning to get in a bad way again. It's hurting me. I don't sleep well at all. I thought it would slow down sooner than this, but I was wrong.

APR
3

Holy Thursday. The chaplain had a service this morning. I'm enjoying feeling close to God. It has been somewhat of a crutch.

In the period, from 3:00 this afternoon to 6:00 this evening, we received three mortar barrages.

NEWS FROM THE U.S....

April 4

Dr. Denton Cooley implants the first temporary artificial heart.

April 29

First anniversary of the Broadway production of the musical *Hair* is celebrated with free concert at Wollman Skating Rink and a "birthday be-in" in New York's Central Park, Sunday 27.

Hair: The American Tribal Love/Rock Musical, by Clive Barnes, is about hippies and was a significant part of the drug, music and peace-love culture of the 1960s. It is famous for originally being performed with all the players totally naked in some scenes. Album sales are one-million copies world-wide.

APR
7

I flew another mission today, dropping propaganda leaflets over the enemy's positions. The leaflets read: "End your attacks and surrender or you will die."

I was flying at five thousand feet, out of small arms fire range, and I dumped out little packs of the leaflets and watched them scatter and fall over the Vietnam jungle. It's kind of beautiful flying over the jungle; everything is such a dark lush green. The crooked, meandering streams all look mud-brown. If I didn't have to worry about being shot at, I could really dig flying here.

No mail recently, no breaks, no change.

APR
8

Rockets hit us at approximately 10:00 P.M. I was stoned when we got hit. I had smoked pot an hour or so before. It's a down and a horror when something scares me.

I smoked two nights ago also and had a pleasant mild experience. I remember smelling the vegetation and wetness in the air.

APR
10

Two weeks ago seem like yesterday and two weeks ahead seem like an eternity. The days go by swiftly, but the months seem to hang around forever.

APR
11

It's been fairly eventful these past couple of days. Last night, we caught about fifteen rockets over by the airstrip.

Yesterday afternoon, I had the sad job of escorting the body of a Vietnamese boy who had set off a Viet Cong booby trap while he was playing near his hamlet. I couldn't tolerate the expression on his mother's face upon learning of her son's senseless death. I wept with her; even so, she hated the sight of me and the other Americans with me. Sergeant So explained my true feelings to her.

Two nights ago, I took a big chance by sneaking off the compound with Alabama. We slinked out in full combat dress, loaded and carrying our rifles as we ventured into town to spend the night with two bar girls who had invited us to spend a night with them. We stole back into camp just before dawn, tired, drunk, hungry, and giggling at the extent of our virile escapade. We are very proud of this caper and often tease and rib the other guys about how well we pulled it off.

APR
18

Today, through a radio news broadcast, I learned that Korea has shot down a United States reconnaissance aircraft. There is trouble in the pot with Korea and the United States. It's the *Pueblo* crisis renewed.

We—and by "we" I mean the people of the world—have all the capabilities of technology, the brilliance, and the sheer stupidity to completely destroy ourselves.

APR
21

I went to town today and had a few beers with some of the guys. When I left the bar, a hooker leaning against a wooden wall caught my attention. She sexily walked over to me and asked me the time of day. I surprised her with my working knowledge of Vietnamese. The temptation became overwhelming. I paid to sleep with her. Today I offended myself, so I also offended God.

I helped spoil the Vietnamese economy by paying that woman five hundred piasters. The average wage of a farmer working his wet, muddy, leech-ridden rice paddies is ninety cents a day. His son can go to town and shine the G.I.s' boots and make upwards of three or four dollars a day. This is partly how our presence is ruining the Vietnamese economy.

APR
22

I have dug up some quotes by Ho Chi Minh, the President of North Vietnam. He is very loved by his people and I'm beginning to understand the intent of the very patient North Vietnamese. "Uncle Ho," as we call him, seems to know exactly what he is doing and I'm sure he realizes the weaknesses within the United States. I personally admire the man.

Man Behind A War: Ho Chi Minh

1. Before the bombing and a half million American troops, Ho said:

"It took eight years of bitter fighting to defeat you French, and you knew the country and had some old friendships here. Now the South Vietnamese regime is well armed and helped by the Americans. The Americans are much stronger than the French, though they know us less well. It may perhaps take ten years to do it, but our heroic compatriots in the south will defeat them in the end."

2. Afterwards, Ho said:

"I think the Americans greatly underestimate the determination of the Vietnamese people. The Vietnamese people have always shown great determination when faced with a foreign invader."

3. *"We are prepared for many years of war."*

APR
23

I realize that I am thinking of things bigger than myself and this is somewhat of a relief.

APR
24

I visited Hoa in town this afternoon. I've known her for a month only and today she spoke of her love for me. She is the purest, saddest female in the world. She really gets prettier every time I see her. I respect her cleanliness. I am her only reason for remaining in Phouc Vinh. I care for her so much.

A 122-mm rocket battalion of the enemy has been spotted in our area of operations.

I have one hundred and thirteen days left in Viet Nam.

I have begun to read *Kon-Tike*.

MAY
4

I've neglected this ledger. But not intentionally.

Another month has passed. I now have one hundred and four days left in Viet Nam. I count the days as most G.I.s do. I shouldn't, though, because it only makes the time drag.

We haven't been hit in nineteen days; it has finally slowed down. Thank you, God, for hearing me speak.

During the past couple of weeks there has been much upset and unrest on the college campuses in the United States. There is a definite revolution going on and only time will reveal its outcome. I don't agree with forceful overthrows, though.

Last week I had a frightful experience with pot. I became so incoherent and scared. What marijuana does, I think, is to intensify a situation or mood. If my disposition is good then it becomes better with pot; if it's bad, then it becomes worse.

I've been seeing Hoa frequently. I'm so damn confused. How can I love so many girls?

I'm really depressed with the Army. I can't stand the loss of identity I have here.

NEWS FROM THE U.S....

A rally and occupation of the Low administrative office building at Columbia University, (planned to protest the university's participation in the Institute for Defense Analysis), is scuttled by conservative students and university security officers. Demonstrators march to Morningside Heights to stage a protest, which eventually results in the occupation of five buildings—Hamilton, Low, Fairweather and Mathematics halls, and the Architecture building. It will culminate seven days later when police storm the buildings and violently remove students and supporters at the Columbia administration's request.

May 11

The New York Times reports a battalion of the 101st Airborne Division climbing Hill 937 in the A Shau found the 28th North Vietnamese Regiment waiting for it.

The fight for "**Hamburger Hill**" raged for ten days and became one of the war's fiercest and most controversial battles. Entrenched in tiers of fortified bunkers with well-prepared fields of fire, the enemy forces withstood repeated attempts to dislodge them. Supported by intense artillery and air strikes, Americans made a slow, tortuous climb, fighting hand to hand. By the time Hill 937 was taken, three Army battalions and an ARVN regiment had been committed to the battle.

May 26

John Lennon and Yoko Ono spend a week in bed at the Queen Elizabeth Hotel in Montreal, Quebec, and record the song "Give Peace a Chance".

MAY
5

I had an experience with monsoon lightning this afternoon. A bolt of electricity wildly struck the tin roof of the hovel I was in. The temporary building shook with the crack of the lightning. It happened at the climax of a daily monsoon shower. Too damn close and mighty powerful.

I spoke with three North Vietnamese prisoners today. They were captured by one of our patrols. There is a definite dissimilarity between the people from North Vietnam and their counterparts from the south. I prefer North Vietnamese over those in the south. Most probably because all the ills of the Americans and all the social dirt connected with war have ruined the South Vietnamese. We spoke of the United States soldiers' operations here in the south, the bombing raids in the north, and the war in general. I have noticed that the North Vietnamese have better teeth than the southerners.

I also learned that since the bombing halt there has been an increase in the supplies coming south to a tremendous degree. They explained the horrible fright they experienced during a B-52 raid.

I finished reading *Kon-Tike.*

MAY
9

Rockets at 9:45 P.M. It has been more than six days without any shelling. It will probably be a long night. More war, damn it.

Today is Momma's birthday. I would like to quote something from Wordsworth and apply it to my mother:

> *"She is the anchor of my purest thoughts, the nurse, the guide, the guardian of my heart, and soul. Of all my moral being....*

> *"Surely I am led by her*

> *"She is not puffed up by false unnatural hopes, nor selfish with unnecessary cures."*

MAY
11

I'm thoroughly disgusted and fed up with the Army. I have to cope with so much harassment from my superiors. I'm sick of Vietnam and its people. Many make asses out of Americans.

I won't be promoted to sergeant because of my attitude. So what? To hell with it all.

I have been turned down for R.& R. twice. I applied a third time. I understand I am allowed to take a seven day leave, though, and I plan to do this. This is quite an opportunity to travel.

MAY
12

Last night we had one hell of a battle. An enemy unit, in human wave style, attacked our base camp. Minutes after they started shooting, our helicopter gunships were up and making thundering passes over the location. We also hit them with small arms, artillery, and air rocket artillery from the gunship choppers. Thankfully, I was not part of base defense that evening. I was a secondary force behind the forward shooting line. The attackers threw some mortars in at the green line aiming at our bunker fortifications. At one point, they managed to cut the out wire and get in, but they were driven back.

The sky was lit up all night and the air rocket artillery from the Cobra gunships and their mini-guns, etc. were hitting hard and frequently. It was a night I won't soon forget. The contact lasted till daybreak. Oddly enough, there were no U.S. casualties.

I was on the patrol that some of the officers and NCO's formed to take a body count. We marched out an hour or so after daybreak. To my front, I saw the charred and burned foliage; some of it was still smoking. The entire area stunk of burnt gunpowder. As we walked closer and approached their farthest penetration point, I could see the twisted and maimed bodies of the attackers.

Some of the dead were strewn across the barbed wire in unbelievable positions. At a closer look, I saw the blood. Some of it was still wet and dripping from their dead cold bodies; some of it was dried and brown on their skin and clothes. The sergeants counted the bodies in a quiet but pleased mood. Many of the G.I.s abused the dead, hunting for souvenirs.

I became nauseous and threw up. My eyes filled with silent tears. Last night, when I saw all this happening, I felt as one does in an arena. I felt the way you do when the Mets are losing a baseball game in late innings, and they suddenly come up from behind, go ahead, and win. I'm ashamed and confused.

One of the dead was a Vietnamese man who was allowed to come into the camp daily to cut our hair. The enemy are all around.

MAY
14

I'm fairly well finished with my loving thoughts of Vietnam. I've been hurt and stepped on too many times.

The Communist forces are continuing their wave of terrorism on the cities and civilian populated areas such as Saigon, Da Nang, and Hue. It's awfully disgusting and churns my stomach. I can't sympathize with North Vietnam any longer.

Another reason for my feeling assured that the United States isn't at fault for intensifying and escalating the war is the fact that the U.S. forces aren't and haven't been attacking enemy-targets except for search-and-clear missions and counterattacks. The enemy is the aggressive force hitting U.S. installations at will. We fight back on his terms, in his own place, and at his own time.

MAY
15

According to the news I receive from the States, the American students are ripping the universities and colleges apart. They are using revolution for social change and it has spread like cancer. I'm sure now that the end products are far from their original thoughts and desires. The ends are not justifying the means.

The American Negro population seems to be ready for another year of militant hostile actions. No good will come of it; it's going to be a long hot summer.

MAY
16

I'm beginning to appreciate so many things which I took for granted before. The color of an apple and the soft shiny beauty of the golden silk in an ear of corn.

MAY
17

I write now in the most bitter and frightened state of my Vietnamese tour.

Two nights ago on the fifteenth of May we got hit. The bunker adjoining mine received a direct round by a delayed fuse 107-mm rocket. It took a young man's life. Snuffed out just as quickly as it takes to say it. Melvin Cowdell is dead. Dead! Miraculously no one else in the bunker was hurt badly.

I can remember Cowdell at Fort Lewis waiting in the same line as I for jungle boot issues. I can remember talking with him on the long boring plane ride from the States. He was there when I was wounded. He's always been around...except now. All I can do is remember his lean, lifeless body.

Cowdell was killed by a delayed fuse, a damn delayed fuse rocket. A delayed fuse is timed to explode after impact. The enemy realize that we have protection from their shelling attacks, so they have set the rockets to penetrate before they detonate.

The bunker Cowdell was in was completely destroyed. The steel overhead roofing split from the impact and came down on him. The round detonated directly over his head. He died in his sleep.

The same thing could happen to any one of us and it's got us all going. I'm so awfully afraid of dying. I want to go home—away from all this.

My attitude and love for Vietnam is decreasing. I'm sick. I love my folks and I love America. I hope my country can catch herself before it's too late.

Ho Chi Minh's birthday is the nineteenth and we're supposed to be attacked. They celebrate like this! I want to live. A captured prisoner of war stated that we would be shelled for ten minutes at 8:00 P.M. and that this would be followed by a major ground assault.

MAY
19

The mood here is extremely tense. I've never experienced anything like it before. Everyone is especially quiet and nervous and has been since Cowdell's death. We are waiting for the attack.

I have been approved to go on leave. I leave my unit on the third of June.

MAY
23

The large ground probe never materialized, at least not as yet. I anxiously await my leave and return home. Vietnam and this war have hurt me deeply and made me bitter. I'm tired, can't get away from it though.

I'm disappointed in myself many times. I don't know why or what causes this. Certainly my future looks fruitful, as long as I'm willing to put some hard work into it. I don't know, it's just this feeling that crops up every now and then.

Eighty-four days left.

MAY
25

We have set up a rat patrol. It's just a joke among the guys. There are so many rats here where we sleep and eat that we have declared war on them. The one who kills the most rats gets a couple of cartons of cigarettes.

MAY
26

Use your body, use your mind, and make the most of all.

MAY
28

Rockets at 7:20 P.M. and again at approximately 10:00. For some strange and uncanny reason it seemed exciting tonight. I was caught out in the open during the first shelling.

The same things that stimulated me a few long months ago no longer do so. The odors in Phouc Vinh were repulsive to me this morning. I noticed how dirty everything is. Including the people.

JUNE
2

I go on leave tomorrow. The compound was hit with rockets just as I was packing my bag.

JUNE
17

TOKYO, JAPAN. Mt. Fuji, Yokahama, the Ginza, and the girl. I had them all.

Well, I've been on leave to Japan and am back. I arrived at Phouc Vinh this afternoon. It has been an exciting adventure.

I saw Saigon. A nasty and crowded oriental city full of armed soldiers. I got drunk with a horde of Australian soldiers at my departing point, and spent a day and a half at Ton Son Shut Airport trying to get a flight out.

I found Japan and the Japanese to be very clean and polite.

There was romance for me in Japan. I met an awfully level-headed and fine Vietnamese girl who is in exile from Vietnam. Her father was the former Minister of Labor in Saigon and he and his family were in constant threat of danger. She told me this condition existed for many honest men in that corrupt government. She spoke of her desire to get to America and make some kind of life for herself other than war.

We had a beautiful seven days together. So busy and eventful. We took pictures from atop Tokyo Tower, we walked the streets at night when they were so bright with neon. We rowed a boat on a quiet lake and talked one sunny afternoon. We ate Japanese food together, laughed, and shared our ideals.

We tired ourselves on our climb up Mt. Fuji. She got a splinter in her finger from the walking stick; I cut it out for her. We slipped on the loose cinders, fell in the ice and snow, and got dirty feet. Her head was on my shoulder as she slept on the train back to Tokyo.

Our kiss on my last evening was beautiful-true and saddening. I had to promise to see her if she does make it to the States.

On my arrival back at my unit today, I learned that Thuy Tien, the girl I was so crazy about two months ago, was killed. She was torn apart by the blast and shrapnel from a land mine which detonated under the bus she and others were riding on. Her sister, along with thirty other civilians, died with her.

How can I believe this?

It's wrong, it's crazy, it's a waste, it's stupid, it's hateful. She was so much.... so much of what I look for.

Sincerely I shall miss her. She took a small part of me with her.

This is really war; dirty, ruthless, and bastardly.

JUNE
18

I'm back-boy, am I back. I've got that same familiar pissed off and discouraged feeling that I've had so many times before. It's caused by my superiors, mainly the operations sergeants. I had forgotten that feeling so quickly. I just can't swallow my pride and keep my mouth shut. I'm not built that way. If someone shits on me in this Army, then dammit. I let him know about it. It usually hurts me in the long run, but I despise taking ridiculous orders from a professional Army man.

I can't stand this. If I'm not worried about getting killed, I have to worry about all this harassment. Am I wrong for bucking it?

I arrived back at Phouc Vinh during the height of the southern monsoon. All the dirt and dust have turned to mud. When I got off the plane at Ton Son Shut Airport, the hot, humid air rushed at me and filled my nose and mouth. I could hardly breathe, I had no desire to. All I could remember was the clean, scented, cool air atop Mt. Fuji. That alone was worth the entire trip.

JUNE 19

A few rounds were pumped in just as a monsoon shower started.

What it all boils down to is the cold, hard fact that some force is trying to kill or injure me and the people around me. When I hear the explosions and feel the concussions, politics has no part in it. This is the end, the bottom station. I often wonder if Washington knows about rockets, mortars, bullets, life, death, and this tremendous suffering.

JUNE 20

I visited a medic this morning to get some relief for my shoulder. It has been paining me more than usual recently. I think the temperature change had a lot to do with this discomfort. He checked me out and scheduled me for a visit to an evacuation hospital in Long Binh soon. If they decide to operate, I will be sent to Japan.

I have had an approval for an R.&R. to Australia next month.

Another base camp not far from here had a huge ground attack last night.

I'm reading *Sayonara*.

JUNE 21

I am twenty-two years old today, but it's not a happy birthday!

JUNE
23

I want so much to make whatever I'm after. I'm thinking such good things. My mind is so much more expanded. I'm trying to understand myself.

I'm still waiting to get out to Long Binh to have my shoulder wound examined.

JUNE
24

So many Vietnamese people are leaving Vietnam because they see, as I do, what the end result will be. A coalition government will mean Communist reign. This is where it's heading. All these young men are dying for nothing.

JUNE
25

God is as powerful as I am.

JUNE
26

I'm finally at Long Binh, the largest military complex in the world.

A doctor X-rayed my shoulder and released me without any medical attention being necessary. I'm visiting two friends of mine who are stationed here. I had a steam bath and a massage here on the post.

Tonight I am safe, but I'm afraid for other U.S. personnel in Vietnam.

JULY
1

I'm back with my unit. I stayed at Long Binh for a few days milking my medical leave. Nobody knows. Nobody seems to care.

JULY
2

There is a coincidental action taking place at Ben Het, an ARVN base camp north of Phouc Vinh. There is a huge enemy concentration attacking the small outpost nightly and we are not sending support. The political reason for this absurdity is the dissention at home which was displayed on Hamburger Hill. At that place, the 101st Airborne Division was deployed to break down the dug-in fortress Charlie had on that hill. Investigations were made, people screamed to Senators, and Washington was pressured.

Although I disagree with the military and what it stands for, I also disagree with the unnecessary waste of young lives because the military cannot take action. Defend or die.

I can't believe how hopelessly mixed up and scrambled the entire situation is.

JULY 3

A new lieutenant was assigned to my unit. He is a helicopter pilot. l was introduced to him and we began speaking of literature. He gave me a copy of *The Prophet* by Kahlil Gibran. I'm amazed, at how many thoughts about life are crammed into this one small book. I wanted to write down so many of the thoughts that I dug in the book but I would have just been recopying the whole thing. I chose to get a copy of my own and carry it with me to re-read whenever I wanted. The lieutenant and myself have the same thoughts concerning the war. I'm refreshed, having had the opportunity to speak with him.

> *"I am the ancient one who resides in your hearts. To love me you must love others."—The Prophet.*

JULY 5

Rockets…but so far away that no one even knew we got hit. That's the way I like it.

JULY 6

Sergeant So has taught me a new song to play on the guitar. He's a fabulous little guy.

So is probably the most well rounded man I have ever met. I'm so glad that I've had him for my friend! He's got high cheekbones and an angular face which appears to have been chiseled out of wood. His black hair falls in neat strands across his head. He is always smiling, showing good white teeth.

For a tiny man, So is absolutely well proportioned from legs to chest. He is intelligent and understanding. I saw this the very first time I saw his oriental eyes.

I should like to mold my intent after Sergeant So, my Vietnamese pal. We shall always be friends.

JULY
7

Again at approximately 6:00 P.M. rockets slammed into Phouc Vinh. They were not close to my position and I was I hardly phased by them at all.

JULY
8
Tuesday.

I'm leaving for Sydney, Australia on Saturday. I'm excited about going, but much more excited about getting home and beginning my real life. I've got something intangible inside me which is begging to come out. It has recently presented itself to me and I must explore it. Something good is there and my wish is that I don't waste it.

My shoulder is giving me pain again.

Sometimes I feel like a scatterbrain because of my varied thoughts and moods. The following are the thoughts I've been occupied with today:

1. Use your body, use your mind; make the most of all.

2. China shall rise in the next two decades, watch it, be careful.

3. How can I ever possibly marry one girl? I love so many of them, each for different reasons too.

4. Never compare women, beauty is nothing to bargain for and true beauty is more than looks.

5. Football is the greatest sport ever played. It's such a test of brains and strength, and that's what men are all about anyway.

JULY
9

A letter to my mother and father, which I have titled:

GRATITUDE

Thank you for my teeth-straight, even, and white.

Thank you for slapping my hand when I bit my nails.

Thank you for paying a few dollars more for my shoes, every time you bought them. My arches did remain perfect.

Thank you for holding me close to you when I cried.

Thank you for teaching me how to punch that mean kid with freckles on his nose.

Thank you for those new and warm pajama Christmases.

Thank you for my health and welfare; I never was hungry.

Thank you for that five dollars to go out that Friday night when it was raining and I was eighteen. That evening was so important to me then.

Thank you for the very latest three-speed bicycle. God, it was sharp!

Thank you for beating me and talking to me.

Thank you for understanding.

Thank you for my brothers and sister.

Remember that silly old car? Thanks for that, too.

Remember that European sports car…?

Thank you.

It's time I go, now that I have had all this.

It certainly is much to work with.

Thank you.

I may write or teach. Someday.

I may go further away, let my hair grow, sit on a foreign shore somewhere to read, then think.

Whatever it may be, it will turn out well, I know; because I am an extension of both of you.

For I am your thought, I am your feelings, I am your child.

Thank you.

JULY
10

I leave for Australia tomorrow.

JULY
16

Sydney, Australia. It's a good feeling to be safe and clean.

Apollo 11: The moonshot, it's incredible! The astronauts really did it. A brand new era was born.

JULY
17

I met a chick last night in a bar. We drank heavily and went to the apartment I rented. She slept with me. We casually said goodbye this morning.

I have found Australians to be very bland and lacking a culture of their own. They are certainly colorful though.

NEWS FROM THE U.S....

July 20

The human race, represented by Neil Armstrong and Buzz Aldrin, lands on the Moon. *Apollo 11* lifted off for the moon on July 16 and returned safely on July 24

> *"That's one small step for [a] man,*
> *one giant leap for mankind"*

July 25

US President Richard Nixon declares the Nixon Doctrine stating that the United States now expects its Asian allies to take care of their own military defense. This was the start of the "Vietnamization" of the war

July 30

US President Richard M. Nixon makes an unscheduled visit to South Vietnam and meets with President Nguyen Van Thieu and with US military commanders

JULY
22

I've just arrived back at the war in Vietnam. I'm hurt and aggravated at mankind, I feel defeated because I give people so much credit for goodness they don't seem to have.

R.&R. is another war, people are battling to slice away the pocket-money weary G.I.s carry naively to R.&R. sites. It's disgusting. Pimps, whores, fast talkers, and all the scum of the earth grab at us.

While I was on R.&R., I met "K" in a discothèque called the Down Under, in the land down under.

I dressed hip that night, trying hard not to look like R.&R. personnel.

I received my share of stares from the girls as I walked in, but I noticed "K" with some female companions.

I asked her to dance…she accepted, and that began my four day affair with her.

We talked and she began to harp quite understandingly about drugs, the war in Viet Nam, people, and me.

She scared me at first, I suspected something, anything. I caught a slight smell of professionalism. I decided to follow it up, though, being very careful with myself. After all, I was out for a good time and seeking a bed partner.

I had some liquor built up inside me, the results of an early start that evening.

An hour or so after midnight, "K" took me to her flat. There was a party going on. People were flaked out on the floor, some were in bed, and others were up and about the untidy little apartment. I should have begun to question her motives then, but she quickly turned me on to a stick of grass and she herself began a long bout with speed. What a freaky chick. I thought. We had decided to go out and dance and groove but wound up in my room. We stayed there that night, and every day and night, until my plane left that next Sunday morning.

All those hours in that room with "K" were sex oriented. I shall never forget.

"K" 's tongue was magic on my body. My navel being her focal point.

Her own body was warm throughout. The feelings and sensations she aroused in me were brought from some place down inside which had been dormant until then. Her mouth was enough to cause these memories which still flush me with heat throughout; but there was more…much more.

Exciting, timeless climaxes, I exploded inside her with fury, force, and beauty.

She exhausted me, elated me, proved to me how much sex is really worth. We shared such variety, it never became dull.

After we had just finished and lay quiet, I admired her young and experienced body. Imagine four days and nights with only an occasional break from her to buy groceries downstairs, where the world was cold and waiting to swallow me up. I still saw a certain hardness in her but wasn't quite sure of anything anymore. I had begun to trust her during our pillow talk.

I still anticipated her motives but put them out of my mind.

When she caressed my chest and stomach orally and put me into the third bardo, I watched her climb into an ecstasy all her own just knowing she caused all this. At times I almost screamed for mercy.

On Sunday the desk rang up at 5:00. My plane left at 7:00

We' made our last love…

I was sad but had faith.

At 6:00 I was in the shower.

By 6:15 I was walking her back to her flat, through dark, romantic, curved, and crooked little Sydney streets.

The new morning sun was coming up.

We parted near her apartment house and I watched her run from me. It seemed strange but I had no time to think. I rushed back, checked out, got a taxi to my destination, got processed, debriefed, and went to convert my money. That was when I found out. SHE ROLLED ME! THE BITCH, THE HUSTLER!

I wanted to hit her, hurt her. She took my money after all we had shared. But there was no time for anything but boarding the plane.

As the ocean disappeared and the Vietnamese jungle began to rush beneath me, I decided to put her out of my mind.

I fastened my seat belt for landing and thought of how I must become more careful and suspicious again. Here my life is at stake, not my money.

As the wheels screeched down on Ton Son Nhut airbase, I looked through the window and watched all the military freight speed by. I laughed out loud-hard. "K" 's time with me was priceless.

JULY
23

I received a welcome back to my unit with 107-mm rockets. I'm always reminded about the war. But I'm going home soon, I can't wait. I found a letter waiting from Tokyo. She wrote to me.

JULY
25

Charge of Quarters tonight.

The Apollo 11 crew has safely returned to earth. The moon-shot was a complete success. I am very proud of the men, their technology, and the country behind it all. It is said to have been the greatest event in history and justly so. My thoughts reflect the same. We are living in a brand new era.

I flew a reconnaissance mission today.

JULY
26

I want to record the thoughts I've been having about God.

I think often of God but not in the way I have been taught. I see God as an infinity, as everything and anything. I see God in myself and others. Sometimes I don't see him and I'm confused.

There are times when I can't even conceive of God, but sometimes God is a reality. He can be love, beauty, hate, anger, pain, sky, soil, sickness, health, water, and apples. The fact that I am searching and not just accepting God means to me that I have found him.

JULY
26

ON DYING

I have seventeen days left In Phouc Vinh with my unit. Last night while I was alone I reread the last letter my parents would send to my APO address. I became so excited for my parents as well as for myself. I thought WOW! In three weeks this will all be past me. I became so happy.

Then I thought of a shocking thing. What happens if I get killed now with so short a time left? It would absolutely wreck Mom and Dad.

I'm afraid to die, yes. I'm even afraid to be hurt in a minor way, but the real hurt for me is for the people back home. I'm most afraid to die because of them. If I am zapped, part of them would be killed also. These are the sickening worries I have. Sometimes I feel like vomiting when I think like this, as I do all too often. God, please speed me back to my home and my people.

I feel as if the trip to Australia took some direction out of me. I was so ultra-sure of myself before I went, now I don't feel so sure. "K", the chick I was with four days out of the seven, is part of this feeling, I'm certain of it.

I'm hoping that I soon regain my new courage. I miss it. Now is the time for God.

I'm absolutely looking forward to seeing Jennifer. Golly, so much lies ahead when I get home.

JULY
28

Anything in excess is strictly taboo. Gluttony is a sin against yourself. While in Australia, I overplayed the role of a hardcore soldier away from home. In that sense I am a pig.

I'm really disgusted with the way I live. I sleep on a dusty blanket spread on the ground, my clothes are never clean, my skin is always sweaty and dirty. Now that I look back, I can't imagine how I lived like this for a year. I'm so glad it's terminating.

I've settled down from the Australia trip. Water under the bridge.

JULY
31

I am Charge of Quarters tonight.

Sometimes I really become afraid of myself. I have so many hang-ups. I'm so inconsistent. My thoughts range from the gutter to the universe. I'm fed up with people.

I'm beginning to realize how screwed-up some people are and I hate it when they impose their ills upon me. I want to go home to be clean and normal.

I'm scared right now when I'm alone. I get nervous and jittery. A lot of pressure is on me. I will be home in two weeks, but right now I still live here with the war. I know all too well that they have enough time to kill me a thousand times in fourteen days.

I'm afraid of going home with some rotten disease from downtown. I'm afraid of going home and not finding what I'm after, whatever that may turn out to be.

I don't want any hassles. I only wish to be left alone so that I may produce. I beg myself that that part of me which is God will build and mold the Dominick Yezzo I desire.

AUG
4

A few rounds came in this evening, but not as close to my position as it has been recently. The war is at a general lull right now; this means that Charlie is setting up once again for maximum damage. There have been large enemy concentrations spotted on operations a few klicks from here outside of Phouc Vinh! It's in the air for another ground attack.

I have seven days left here with my unit.

I'm going to miss Sergeant So when I leave here. He has been a great deal of help to me in trying times.

I smoked pot last night and became really mellow and placid. I enjoyed music from my radio, and thinking and grooving. I slept well for a change, too. Woke up this morning feeling eager and ready to face the day.

Lately, though, I haven't been sleeping well at all. I've been having WAR nightmares. I wake up screaming No, No!! I dreamt that a rocket just hit my bunker and the thing caved in on me.

Hold on, folks, I'm coming.

AUG
8

I'm nervous and sick with it. I'm not right, haven't been for the past week. I've got tonsillitis and can't seem to shake it. I'm all bunched up inside, scared. Thinking about dying right now. God help me!

I don't know why I allow myself to get like this now. I am so close to the end that I can hardly stand it. Will it all change in seven days? I'll be home by then. God, I hope so. What's happening to me?

I smoked pot a couple of nights ago and got freaky and scared of the war and the misused power mankind possesses.

I'm being given a hard time by the operations sergeant.

It's been quiet for the past month or so but there is a reason for this according to military intelligence. Tay Ninh, Loc Ninh, and An Loc are three areas close to here which are supposed to receive heavy enemy attack from the 9th Viet Cong Division and smaller subordinate divisions.

Essentially, what's going on is one last big push in one or all three of the areas mentioned. The enemy objective is to overrun and take a Provincial Capital, quickly call a ceasefire with Paris before U.S. forces have a chance to regain lost ground, and then set up a Communist government within the limits of South Vietnam.

Five enemy surrenderers have walked into the compound in a very short time, all stating the location of the 9th V.C. Division to be below An Loc. It could be a diversion. When and if the next major assault does come off (which is supposed to be within the next four or five days), I'm sure there will be a series of diversionary attacks at other locations. This could be the end of it—or it could be just another beginning. Recently there have been numerous bombings at suspected enemy positions. The 1st Air Cavalry has had all bombing missions diverted to our area of operations.

God, protect everyone.

AUG
9

ALERT-Phouc Vinh and Song Be may get possible ground attacks.

AUG
10

This is my last day to spend with my unit. God willing, I should be home in a few days. I'm not as excited as I'd like to be. I'm kind of leery about going home.

I leave tomorrow but tonight I'm still here.

AUG
11

I was airlifted to Bien Hoa this morning. Last night we had an incoming ground attack. I almost went crazy my last night out there and BAMB-it was an all night shootout. Charlie fought past the guard bunkers at one position and got into the base camp. There were still enemy inside the barbed wire when I hastily boarded the chopper this morning.

I hated parting with Sergeant So that way. I shall always pray for his welfare. Alabama is traveling home with me.

NEWS FROM THE U.S....

3 days of peace and music

"The New York State Thruway is closed", rang out on the news reports, there were 20 miles of traffic jams in all directions for the Woodstock Music Festival.

About 186,000 tickets sold, 200,000 expected, but on Friday night, fences came down, a free concert declared, 500,000 attended the concert on a 600 acre dairy farm.

Police overwhelmed by the numbers but heralded the calm: 2 deaths, 2 births, no reports of burglary or *violent* crime.

> *"These people are really beautiful. There has been no violence whatsoever which is really remarkable for a crowd of this size."—medical officer Dr Wm Abruzzi*

> *"You have proven something to the world...that half a million kids can get together for fun and music and have nothing but fun and music."—dairy farmer Max Yasgur*

Among the many songs of anti war sentiment, talk of free love, nude swimming, and open drug sharing, Joni Mitchell's song "Woodstock" became the symbol of the Woodstock culture:
> *"We were half a million strong*
> *And everywhere there was song and celebration*
> *And I dreamed I saw the bombers*
> *Riding shotgun in the sky*
> *And they were turning into butterflies*
> *Above our nation"*

AUG
12

Bien Hoa.

A couple of rocket rounds landed real close to me. They scared the hell out of me. I'm almost finished processing out.

AUG
15

Long Bien—hit this morning with mortars. They woke me up. I depart some-time today.

AUG
16

It's all over, my war is finished. I felt real sad about parting with my friends. We went through so much together.

I'm on my way back to the United States right now. Flying on a huge Air Force C-141. I cannot help but look back over all that's happened to me in the past year. All the hurt and suffering, all the stupidity and pity I saw, all the good I remember. There were many wonderful and new experiences in that small for-eign land. I shall never forget the Vietnamese.

Now it's all past, the good and the bad, and I'm going home to my family, Jennifer, and school. I pray that my mind and head remain the same and that I build myself into what I want to be.

I'm truly sorry for all the dead young men I leave behind. I made it and they didn't. Why…?

Thank you, Lord, for keeping me.

Epilogue

All war is wrong. Perhaps this latest one is less wrong than others, but still, in all, the US is oppressing Iraq. "The bad guy must go."

All classes alike agree Sadam Hussein is regarded with the likes of Stalin and Hitler; powers of ill and evil…temperaments of self-grandeur…their wills achieved through terror and torture. Men like Sadam Hussein hold contempt for the achieved order of the world, promote anarchy and pay for continued terror with the wealth stolen the force they accomplish.

Death in war is the same now as it always has been; no difference that the Romans lost a life in battle by getting hit in the head with a boulder from a giant sling on wooden wheels or the Americans lost a life in battle by a shell detonating on impact after being precisely guided in the jet engine of a super sonic stealth bomber. Life—which has a sacred base—is lost.

I speak of each life rather than the statistics of lives.

978-0-595-39250-6
0-595-39250-4

CPSIA information can be obtained
at www.ICGtesting.com
Printed in the USA
FSHW011718061020
74471FS

9 780595 392506